Ripe Fields

Ripe Fields

*The Promise and Challenge
of Latino Ministry*

Juan M.C. Oliver

Church Publishing
NEW YORK

Unless otherwise noted, the Scripture quotations contained herein
are from the *New Revised Standard Version* Bible, copyright © 1989
by the Division of Christian Education of the National Council of
Churches of Christ in the U.S.A. Used by permission. All rights
reserved.

              Library of Congress Cataloging-in-Publication Data
Oliver, Juan M. C.
Ripe fields : the promise and challenge of Latino ministry / by Juan
M.C. Oliver.
      p.   cm.
Includes bibliographical references.
ISBN 978-0-89869-611-0 (pbk.)
1. Church work with Hispanic Americans—Episcopal Church.
2. Hispanic American Episcopalians—Religious life. I. Title.
BX5979.5.H57O45 2009
283'.7308968--dc22
                                    2009002696

Cover image courtesy of Superstock / © suravid
Cover design by Lindy Gifford
Interior design by Vicki K. Black

Printed in the United States of America

Church Publishing, Incorporated
445 Fifth Avenue
New York, New York 10016

www.churchpublishing.com

5   4   3   2   1

For Johnny Lorenzo

Table of Contents

Acknowledgments

Many people have supported the ministry of this Latino, encouraging, critiquing, nurturing, and demanding of me, but never condescending or despairing of my abilities. There are more than I can name. But let me try.

My family made me Latino as well as a Christian over my first seventeen years of life in Puerto Rico. Without their culture and faith I would not be me. The Jesuits further formed me in the faith and gave me a venue to exercise my culture's respect for the intellectual life in the midst of a new, exciting, and sometimes exasperating Anglo culture. They served as a cultural incubator, allowing me a safe space in which to learn Anglo ways without going crazy at the unpredictability of English prepositions.

In the Episcopal Church, Michael Merriman was first to treat me like an intelligent liturgist. Joe Morris Doss and Clay Morris egged me on to courageously rethink our inherited liturgical practices as I deepened my understanding of the Christian community and its symbolic system in the years following seminary. Later on Joe also greatly supported the development of Latino ministry in the Diocese of New Jersey.

More recently, the Latino faculty and students at General Seminary's Latino program, which I directed from 1999 to 2008, have been a source of joy and hope in the future of Latino ministry in the United States and beyond. They include José Luis Lana, Julio Torres, Rebeca Radillo, Efraín Agosto, Carla Roland-Guzmán, Jorge Samayoa, Gladys Díaz, Loyda Morales, Antonio Checo, Luis Gómez, and José L. Martínez. Beyond General Seminary, I am particularly grateful to Justo González, Wilfrido Ramos-Orench, Anthony Guillén, and Gloria del Castillo for their dedication and support.

Over the last two years my research for this book was greatly enhanced by grants from the Conant Foundation and the Seminary Consultation on Mission, which allowed me to travel extensively in Latin America to assess the reality of theological education of Anglican seminarians in that continent.

Many thanks also to Frank Tedeschi and Vicki Black, wonderful editors who patiently encouraged, prodded, and supported this project.

Finally, my deepest gratitude goes to the Council of the Associated Parishes for Liturgy and Mission. This group of thirty friends and colleagues deeply concerned with the relationship between the church's worship and its mission has been a source of joy, sanity, and unwavering support for this Latino Episcopalian for more than twenty years.

Introduction

> Do you not say, "Four months more, then comes
> the harvest"? But I tell you, look around you, and
> see how the fields are ripe for harvesting. The
> reaper is already receiving wages and is gathering
> fruit for eternal life, so that sower and reaper may
> rejoice together. For here the saying holds true,
> "One sows and another reaps." I sent you to reap
> that for which you did not labor. Others have
> labored, and you have entered into their labor.
> (John 4:35–38)

There is a growing interest in Latino ministry in the Episcopal Church, partly the result of an increasing awareness of the accelerated growth of the Latino population in the United States. Indeed, demographers tell us that in another forty years, Hispanics will constitute almost a third of the population of the United States. What is the Episcopal Church planning to do to respond to this challenge in evangelism? So far the answer is not clear. Despite strong statements by Latino bishops, such as the Atlanta Manifesto, and the good will of hundreds of clergy and laity across the nation, the Episcopal Church still does not have a national plan for the development of Latino ministry.

In the midst of various challenges resulting in the Episcopal Church's membership decline, our church also faces the unprecedented opportunity to embrace the changing times with excitement, zeal, and hope. The dramatic increase in the numbers of Latinos/Hispanics in communities throughout the country should be seen as an evangelistic opportunity and hope for the church. As the report by the 20/20 task force put it in 2001, "Such radically changing demographics should encourage the church to be courageous, resourceful, passionate, and enthusiastic in its response to these new circumstances." — *Creating a Welcoming Presence*

This modest book intends to contribute to that development by presenting an overview of the great promise and challenge of Latino ministry facing the Episcopal Church today. Moreover, although I write from an Episcopal context, I believe this promise and challenge affects—both positively and negatively—the wider ecumenical church, across denominations.

My goal here is not to present a development plan, but to examine a phenomenon that has been taking place in Latino ministry for at least the last twenty-five years: it seems that as we meet the ongoing challenges in Latino ministry development we are unable to grow as a result of our experience, so we tend to repeat the same mistakes over and over. This aspect of Latino ministry puzzles even the most well-intentioned promoters of ministry among this growing population.

The reader may well ask why this book on Latino ministry is written in English. I could have written it in Spanish, but its readership would have been unable to do much to address the challenges before us. The reason for this is that Latino ministry in American churches is still largely in the hands of non-Latino, Anglo-Saxon clergy and laity. This book is therefore addressed to those Anglo leaders in American churches, who are facing what is possibly the greatest challenge in mission and evangelism in their history.

So I write here in English about Latino ministry in the United States, its challenges and immense promise. The stories and ideas in this book arise from twenty-five years of living with this challenge and promise, and from my perception that there are recurring patterns in Latino ministry crying out to be identified and named. It is my belief that in order to reap the ripe harvest in the fields we must first take a good look at the harvest, naming and grappling with its idiosyncrasies and cultural specificities. We cannot go out to harvest beans expecting them to be wheat. Our efforts will succeed only if we acknowledge that this harvest is different, that the harvesting methods we have employed before may not work in this terrain and with this crop, and that we need to know much more about these fields in order to welcome them into the granary of the reign of God.

Using short vignettes as a starting point of each chapter, I present a series of situations related to Latinos in the church. These stories show both the ingrained obstacles that prevent the church from developing this increasingly crucial ministry in the United States and the opportunities before the church to engage in this ministry in a successful way across every aspect of its common life. The book is structured "from the bottom up," beginning with the congregational development of Latino churches and moving on to Christian formation, questions of authority and stewardship, ordination and ministry, diocesan oversight, and theological education. I end with a visionary story about a Latino congregation that is implementing many of the ideas presented throughout the book.

Although every chapter in this study begins with an anecdote, this is not a work of fiction. The stories presented at the beginning of each chapter are true and actually took place, though in some I have combined characters and situations. In all of the stories I have changed names, genders, and places in order to protect the players from either shame or fame.

CHAPTER 1

Who is Latino?

A group of church leaders gathered around the coffee pot during a break at a national church conference. We all knew each other well, and soon we were bantering and joking. I said something about being Latino.

"Oh sure, Juan, but you're not really Latino," someone said. I pointed to my white skin and began my usual explanation about Latinos including the whole gamut of skin coloration.

"No, no," he stopped me. "I mean, you're not Latino," he said innocently. "Your parents went to college and you have a doctorate!"

Even after I reminded him, indignantly, that minorities have a right to name themselves and not be defined by members of the majority, he insisted. That's when I realized that we live in two different worlds, friends though we are.

I went home furious after this exchange. I had just been exiled from my people for not fitting an Anglo stereotype of who we are! My friend thought that I was less Latino because I have had the benefits of education. Apparently he is not aware of other educated Latinos in the United States and Latin America. Or perhaps by "Latino" he meant only the stereotypical immigrant of recent years—a poor, relatively uneducated person driven north by violence or chronic poverty. That would leave out hundreds of thousands of Latinos in the United States who are educated, many of whose forebears were here almost a century before Captain Smith fell in love with Pocahontas at Jamestown.

We need to know to whom we are speaking,
even in a general sense, before we know
how best to communicate.
—*Creating a Welcoming Presence*

What do we mean by "Hispanic" and "Latino"? What's in a name? I bring this up at the start because names are extremely important. They are markers or signs that summarize our sense of self and others. We therefore begin our journey by examining whether we should call ourselves Latinos or Hispanics, as well as the stereotypical meanings that these terms may have for the dominant culture. We will then explore Hispanic demographics in the United States in order to get a sense of the pressing need to develop proactive missionary strategies to welcome Latinos into the Episcopal Church. Finally, we will examine what we mean in the church by "Latino ministry."

WE ARE LATINOS

The church often speaks of ministry among Hispanics, but in fact this is not what we call ourselves. "Hispanic" is a category invented by the U.S. Census Bureau to tag persons of Spanish or Latin American ancestry living in the United States. Of course the term covers us all, but that is not what we call ourselves. In Spanish, the term *Hispano/a* is an adjective describing a person or thing related to Roman Hispania, the Iberic peninsula in Europe. Most Latin American countries, however, declared their independence from Spain in the early 1800s, and in spite of the fact that we sometimes refer to it with a dash of irony as the "Motherland," we have long stopped considering ourselves related to Spain, thanks to Morelos, Bolívar, and other independence leaders in Latin America almost two hundred years ago. We are not *Hispanos*. We are *Latinos*. That's what we call ourselves.

Many Anglos do not realize that Latin America is comprised of *all* the countries on the American continents (North and South) which lie south of the Rio Grande, with the addition of Caribbean countries such as Cuba, Dominican Republic, and Puerto Rico. All these nations were colonized by European nations whose languages developed from Latin, and thus in the nineteenth century the French developed the term *Amérique Latine* to refer to them. Thus people from countries as distant and dis-

7

tinctive as Brazil and Puerto Rico, Mexico, Colombia and Argentina all identify themselves as Latinos.

The Hispanic/Latino community is complex and multileveled. . . . With over forty years of on-the-ground experience, we recognize that there [are] many different and particular communities, each with its own historical, regional, and cultural identity. —*Creating a Welcoming Presence*

As Latinos, our cultural identity was shaped by our centuries-long experience of colonization and racial admixture. We are united by a common language and a shared history of colonial invasions, exploitation, genocide, and chronic poverty, all visited upon us at times in the name of God. We may have different countries of origin, and these will determine our culinary tastes and our slang, but there is something much more powerful that unites us as a people. In light of this common background, we can talk about a Latin American "identity," carried over by Latinos in the United States well after we become bicultural and bilingual "over there."

The only "Hispanics" in the United States who might not fit this description are the descendants of Spaniards who colonized the southwestern United States in the sixteenth century. Forgotten by Mexico and sold to the United States for a pittance, these *Hispanos* from Texas to California have managed to maintain, nourish, and develop a vibrant culture with roots in Spanish, Mexican, and, increasingly since the late nineteenth century, Anglo cultures.

Thus, although the dominant culture in the United States insists on describing us as Hispanics, often meaning by that merely a collection of stereotypes, we do not see ourselves that way. Yet we are partly to blame for this stereotyping. In the wake of the civil rights movement, we have been tempted to define ourselves in terms of race rather than our unifying culture. It is much easier and convenient to tag as "Hispanic" some measurable, tangible attributes, such as skin tone or accent, but "Hispanic" and "Latino" do not actually refer to either the color of our skin or our accent, nor to our educational level, but to our shared *culture*. Our shared culture and all the subcultural elements that comprise it through a large and very varied region have, over the centuries, integrated these differences into a shared sense of unity.

Some Latinos certainly do experience discrimination on account of their race, be it black, Native American, mestizo, or mulatto. But this is not the whole story. "Latino" is a much broader category—a category related more to the ways in which we live, move, and have our being than to our race, education, or income. It is a category that includes a multiplicity of races, all living out of the same Latin American cultural matrix. A person who discriminates against a Latino may or may not be racist— it depends on that Latino's race. Thus it is not racism *per se* that is at stake, but Anglo *ethnocentrism,* the natural tendency of humans who can only live, move, and have their being in *only one way.* "Our way" naturally is "the only way" and we assume that the whole world is this way, or should be.

As Latinos in the United States, we labor daily within and outside the pigeonholes set by the dominant culture's stereotypical classification. Sometimes we return the favor. The pigeonholes are legion; here are some examples.

ANGLO STEREOTYPES OF LATINOS	LATINO STEREOTYPES OF ANGLOS
"Latinos are all Roman Catholics."	"Anglos are all Protestants."
"Latinos are lazy."	"Anglos are workaholics."
"Latinos are overemotional."	"Anglos repress feelings."
"Latinos are aggressive."	"Anglos are passive aggressive."
"Latinos can't be good administrators."	"Anglos are efficient robots."

Recent studies show that the population of the United States is undergoing a shift away from an Anglo-dominant nation toward a truly multicultural one. Additionally, whereas earlier immigration patterns involved assimilating into Anglo-American culture in a kind of melting pot, more recent immigrants tend to retain their cultural and linguistic identity even as they acculturate to the dominant culture by learning Anglo ways. This trend will probably result in an increasingly large proportion of the population of the United States becoming bilingual and bicultural.

In 2004 the Census Bureau announced that the nation's Hispanic and Asian populations would triple over the next half-century. Non-Hispanic whites, who in 1960 made up 85 percent of the population and are now about two-thirds, will become a minority when their share drops to 47 percent by 2050. Hispanics, on the other hand, who are already the largest minority group, will more than double their share of the population to 29 percent by 2050.

Fundamental to the identity of the Episcopal Church is its welcoming and hospitable environment. There is room for persons of different theological and doctrinal positions within the Episcopal Church, just as there is room for persons of different class backgrounds.... Such hospitality needs to extend to persons who are different from most of the members of the Episcopal Church. This hospitality flies in the face of the xenophobia increasing in the U.S. This hospitality proclaims the gospel in a countercultural way, demonstrating to the rest of society that God cares for all persons, no matter their legal status, their sins, their color.

—*Creating a Welcoming Presence*

The growth of the Latino population of the United States thus continues apace. Latino immigration, "legal" or not, surged during the Reagan administration's *Contra* wars of the 1980s and has grown to the point that demographers tell us that new immigrants and their children and grandchildren born in the United States will account for 82 percent of the population increase from 2005 to 2050. This is not the place to ask why; that is for historians and economists to ferret out. The undeniable fact, however, is that the Latino population of the United States is growing by leaps and bounds. We are everywhere. Additionally, although current trends find the number of American-born Latinos to be growing faster than immigrating Latinos, immigration from Latin America, propelled by the great economic chasm that separates us from the rest of the Americas, will not likely decrease any time soon, at least not until Latin American economies begin to pull out of the stagnation to which they have been condemned by five hundred years of exploitation.

Thus the growing presence of Latinos in the United States is neither a temporary trend nor a small detail that we can afford to ignore. It presents possibly the greatest missionary challenge to the churches in the United States in their history. It also holds great promise.

LATINO EPISCOPALIANS

Based upon our experience, Latinos in the Episcopal Church also face a challenge: to develop our theology as a reflection upon our experience of God from within our own cultural context *and* within the wider context of an Anglican tradition. We have taken great strides in the last decade. One area of success is the location of our theology firmly in the Latino experience of poverty and privation, which are rightly for us a place of God's revelation. This insight connects Latino theologians in the United

States with Latin American theological movements of the last thirty years.

> In one way or another, either because of work, lifestyle, discrimination, or past experience, our potential members feel "out of touch" or "out of place" at church. They are looking for a place to make their own choices and build their own faithful and religious identity.
>
> —*Creating a Welcoming Presence*

But Latinos in the United States, unlike our counterparts in Latin America, have another experience, which to my knowledge has not yet been named as a place of divine revelation: our experience of learning another culture—Anglo culture. Like poverty, our experience of learning a second culture is a theological gold mine. Once we are "over here" (sometimes even before we arrive), Latinos spend most of our time learning Anglo ways. For instance, we learn, slowly and patiently, the myriad ways in which the verb "to get" can be combined with prepositions to mean almost anything. We learn that life is possible without subjunctives. We learn to tell time in a different way from ours. We learn that people here are individuals, and that the family has usually just four people if you are lucky. We learn that religion is a matter of free choice and that "if you can think it, you can do it." We learn that it is possible to be "a self-made man." We learn that "net worth" is a dollar amount, not a feeling inside—what we would call *honor*. We learn that here being poor is an indication of God's displeasure with you, as taught by the

13

Calvinist colonizers of this land who consider poverty a manifestation of God's judgment or of personal moral failure.

In short, since we spend all our time learning Anglo culture, most Latinos with a few years' experience in the United States—even Latinos with very little education—are experts in multicultural ministry. We minister constantly to people of a different culture from ours: clean their homes, care for their children, pick their vegetables—some of us even teach their seminarians and grade their term papers. So I suggest that we include the experience of learning to be bicultural as a rich place of revelation where God is present and manifest.

God is manifest in our bicultural experience by bursting the bubble of the dominant culture's claims to be final arbiter and universal standard of everything. Once the bubble has been burst, we discover that our experience of learning Anglo ways reveals to us something about God and life that we did not know before—something that forms us as immigrants and our descendants as a people, and that makes us who we are as immigrants to the United States: *Anglo culture is not God.*

Precisely because we have survived and thrived through the process of learning a second culture, we have discovered that culture and its components—language, manners, rituals, body language—is *multiplex.* We have discovered that the world created by a given culture for those in it is only *one* world among *other* worlds. Our experience thus reveals that there are many ways of being in the world, not only our way, and that each way builds up its own world with its traditions, assumptions, values, virtues, and sins. The bicultural person knows—from actual experience, not merely in theory—that "the way things are" is many ways, and that there are other ways of doing whatever must be done "just this way."

Thus, the immigrants' place of revelation is also a place of dangerous knowledge, for in the eyes of monocultural people, our "other" ways of doing things undermine the stability of their world. This insight may throw light on the recent nasty dialogue about immigration. It is no wonder that we, who have found out that the world has room for many ways of being, are considered best as being ministered *to,* even *managed,* for monocultural members of the dominant culture are sensitive enough to feel that if we "others" are permitted to act out our world, we may well construct and express a different world from theirs with a different order of power and meaning. Naturally, this is profoundly threatening to them.

As Latino "others," we might paint the church in loud colors. Or insist that there cannot be worship without offering something (candles, flowers, ex-votos) to God. We might need to be accompanied in worship by the saints, the church triumphant. We might develop a long entrance rite to allow everyone to arrive before the first reading. We might express our respect of the dignity of the poor and give them pride of place in our assemblies. We might insist that the two-track system of preparation for ordination (Commission on Ministry followed by seminary) be integrated into a single track so that the seminary's daily experience of the ordinand can be part of his or her discernment process. We might consider practical work in field education parishes every bit as creditable as academic work in the classroom, finding new ways of integrating one into the other and keeping the two experiences in dialogue. We might decide that since there are so few Latinos with undergraduate degrees, our seminary education must seek ways of assisting promising candidates to complete their bachelor's degree while starting their graduate education in theology. These are just a few creative examples. Clearly, Latinos who are *doing* rather than *receiving* ministry are a dangerous lot.

As members of a very wide and rich cultural matrix, Latinos in the United States daily juggle the task of valuing and retaining our culture while learning the dominant Anglo culture. We do this in the midst of stereotypical misunderstandings of who we are and where we come from. This book attempts to clarify and correct some of these misunderstandings, in order to remedy the series of false starts to which Latino ministry in the United States seems condemned, even while our numbers continue to grow.

WHICH LATINO?

Years ago, while I was discerning my vocation to the priesthood, I called a bishop in a heavily Latino diocese. An affable man, he showed some interest in developing Latino congregations near the Mexican border. "Where are you from?" he eventually asked.

"I'm Puerto Rican," I explained, "and moved to the States when I was seventeen."

Silence. Then, as kindly as he could, he said, "I wish you well, but I'm not looking for Puerto Ricans; I need Mexican clergy."

The ignorance of Latino cultures evidenced by this statement is impressive. The bishop assumed that different nationalities make different Latin Americans unable to minister to each other. But we must ask, can an Anglo-American priest serve in an Australian congregation? Can a French-Canadian work with people in France? Can a Venezuelan relate to Peruvians? The historical answer to all these questions is a clear *yes*. The idea that differences in Latin American countries of origin and their subcultures make Mexicans, Puerto Ricans, Bolivians, Venezuelans, Argentineans, and so on incompatible with each other is extremely naïve. Each of these countries of course has its own slang, cuisine, and idiosyncratic ways of expressing and viewing the world, but they are all part of a broader Latin American culture, so that as a result, Latinos have much more in common *with each other* than with Anglos in North America. Sometimes recent immigrants from Latin America, thrown together in church for the first time with members from other countries, will be shocked by the differences among Latinos. This is entirely natural. In a short time, however, they will discover our commonalities and shared culture, and will soon be joking about differences in slang and cuisine.

The rate at which our presence in the United States is growing is nothing short of impressive. Latinos already constitute the largest minority in the United States and in forty more years will likely reach a third of the population. This presents a tremendous missionary challenge and promise to the mainstream churches, *one that can be met only by getting to know Latinos as we actually are.*

This depth and honesty of relationship with us, however, cannot take place as long as we continue to gloss over the differences between Anglo and Latino languages and cultures, pretending that we are all the same, in some well-intentioned but naively mistaken quest for peaceful inclusion. The unity of different peoples in the church cannot be bought by sacrificing our diversity; rather, that unity will be realized only when we recognize *and welcome* our differences as reflections of the life of our Creator, who is one, while consisting of three distinct persons. With this caveat in mind, we turn first to the development of Latino congregations.

CHAPTER 2

Latinos in Church: Congregational Development

*Bishop Johnson called her Canon to the Ordinary. "Larry,"
she said, "did you say you had a resume from a Latino
priest—a former Roman Catholic who wanted to explore
crossing the Thames?"*

*"Oh yeah," Larry said. "This guy, Jorge Méndez, from
Colombia, has been hanging around St. Stephen's and the
rector there says he would make a good priest."*

*Bishop Johnson was ecstatic. She owed the rector of St.
Stephen's a favor, and besides, she was tired of showing up
at meetings with other bishops where she could not brag
about having "Hispanic ministry" in her diocese. It was
high time to open a Hispanic congregation.*

"Why don't you bring him in and let me talk to him," she said, and Larry did as ordered.

Months passed, during which Jorge Méndez, whose English was passable at best, was told to read about Anglican worship and theology, and a little bit about history. He was put under the tutelage of a senior priest, Father Billings, who had a doctorate in New Testament and who spoke no Spanish.

Eventually Jorge was received in the Episcopal Church as a priest. In the meantime, however, Bishop Johnson had no idea where to put him. Suddenly one morning she realized that St. Peter's, a former parish (now a small mission) located in a primarily Polish neighborhood that was on the edge of a heavily Latino neighborhood, would have to fold unless it could find new life. A young and energetic priest was just the ticket, and she assigned Father Jorge as vicar of St. Peter's.

Father Jorge exhausted himself developing a Spanish Mass, and fending off the anger of the vestry—mostly Anglo old-timers who felt increasingly threatened by the growing power of the three or four Latino families who were beginning to attend and who almost filled the entire worship space, which seated less than eighty worshippers. Three years later, Father Jorge was suddenly told by the diocesan budget committee chairman that there simply were no funds for supporting his Latino ministry. Before he knew it, Father Jorge was out of a job. He had a congregation of fifty souls, who disbanded soon after he left.

This anecdote is a typical example of how some bishops have gone about developing Latino congregations. Although the Episcopal Church has been officially trying to foster Latino ministry at the national level for the last thirty years or so (before that Latino ministry was up to local bishops) we still have only about three hundred Latino worshipping communities in the United States. Why has the growth been so slow?

> Then Jesus went about all the cities and villages, teaching in their synagogues, and proclaiming the good news of the kingdom, and curing every disease and every sickness. When he saw the crowds, he had compassion for them, because they were harassed and helpless, like sheep without a shepherd. Then he said to his disciples, "The harvest is plentiful, but the laborers are few; therefore ask the Lord of the harvest to send out laborers into his harvest." *(Matthew 9:35–38)*

Some of the clues to this "failure to thrive" may be seen in our story. First of all, Bishop Johnson made the mistake of beginning with a single priest, rather than with a neighborhood with a high concentration of Latinos. Additionally, she seemed to think that "ministry" is something done by clergy *to* the laity, and she therefore naturally waited to have a Latino priest on her hands to begin the project.

But this understanding belies the nature of Christian ministry, to which all Christians are called by virtue of our belonging to the Body of Christ. Jesus asks his disciples to pray that God will send more laborers into the harvest (Matthew 9:37–38), but he is not talking about needing more clergy. He is talking about members of his *kahal,* assembly, or *ecclesia*—those who are called together by God to manifest among them the first fruits of the God's reign. Once gathered, they are sent to gather the grain and bring it into the granary of God's reign—a new world order characterized by justice and peace.

In light of the New Testament understanding of the ministry of all Christians, we cannot continue to think of congregational development as a clergy deployment project. Rather, as Leonardo Boff coined the term, congregational development is *ecclesiogenesis*—gestating an assembly or community of worship and witness. This is best done "from below."

Another reason for the slowness of growth in Latino congregations among us is the cultural isolation and naiveté of monocultural church leaders. As we have seen, in another forty years the Hispanic population in the United States is expected to *triple.* Unless the Episcopal Church moves proactively to develop new congregations that reflect the ethnic diversity of Americans today, it will be relegated to the role of a culturally closed society—an Anglo religious ghetto—for the rest of the century.

In this chapter we will examine the two most common ways we tend to develop Latino congregations in the Episcopal Church today. The first is to start a new congregation "from scratch." This congregation is developed with the expectation that it will one day stand independently as a Latino mission or parish. The second approach is to "nest" a Latino congregation within an existing English-speaking parish, with varying levels of interaction and communication between them.

STARTING FROM SCRATCH

Stage 1: Identifying a location and lay leaders
The natural place to explore the creation of a Latino worshipping community is a neighborhood with a large concentration of Latinos. (I would suggest at least 35 percent.) Assuming that there are no Latino congregations already present in the neighborhood, the bishop might choose to create a Latino Development Task Force, made up preferably of a majority of Latinos who can advise the bishop and the Diocesan Council about Latino realities. Members of this task force should research the demographic data available to the diocese, and not just settle for word-of-mouth information. "But there are no Latinos around here!" often expresses wishful thinking rather than accurate demographic data. We can be invisible to the dominant culture.

Using this more factual information, task force members can then *walk* a likely neighborhood with a high percentage of Latinos, meeting several crucial people: Latino members of the Chamber of Commerce, the police and fire departments, community organizers, city council leaders, and so on. The task force might hold a series of meetings with them to explore the dreams and needs of the neighborhood. In this way the task force members will be able to spot a good location for a Latino church in the neighborhood, a location characterized by heavy foot traffic and accessed by good public transportation. It may be a home, a business that is willing to host a weekly prayer meeting, or a rentable modest space. It may also be an existing church—Episcopal or not—but the task force members should know that this can raise unforeseen problems down the line, as we shall see later.

In the story about Bishop Johnson's efforts to establish a Latino church, St. Peter's was not a likely location for a healthy Latino congregation. The neighborhood was mostly Polish, and with a seating capacity of only eighty worshippers, the church building would never be able to be home to a congregation of five hundred pledging units necessary, as we shall see below, to make a Latino parish economically self-sufficient. Economic self-sufficiency, as we shall see in the chapter on administration and stewardship, is a desirable sign of congregational maturity among Latinos as well as Anglos.

By getting to know the local leaders of the neighborhood, the members of the task force are likely to meet other interested leaders from the community who are willing to engage in the project. By leaders, I mean, of course, people who are already leading the neighborhood, either by nature of their profession (city councilors, policemen, firefighters, social workers, business leaders) or by virtue of their gifts and commitment. These latter are most easily spotted by noticing who people are following or referring matters to, whose names come up in conversation, and who are listened to by others. They may or may not be Episcopalians, and they may or may not be in need of "Anglicanization."

Once a location and a handful of potential leaders have been identified, members of the task force or a Latino Christian trained in facilitating Bible reflection groups may host a weekly Bible reflection meeting there. Note that I say Bible *reflection* rather than Bible *study*. The Bible Reflection Group is a sharing group rather than a class on Scripture. Its leader is a facilitator rather than a teacher. (An example of a Bible reflection group meeting is provided in Appendix A.) The distinction is important because Bible reflection is life-oriented, rather than an academic or intellectual undertanding. Bible reflection leads to conversion. Although Bible reflection is an excellent way for Anglos as well as Latinos to make the biblical text their own and to reflect theologically upon their own experience, Latino cultures in particular value relationships. The Bible reflection group, being a group process and not simply an individual growth program, fits with the Latino understanding of the relational basis of all identity and meaning.

The small group of leaders grapple with the biblical text and reflect on the meaning of their life experiences in the light of Scripture. Soon enough the group will begin to articulate their own sense of call and mission. The specifics can still be very sketchy: "We are trying to follow Jesus and so maybe we should volunteer at the hospital, visiting Latino patients, especially those who are without family." They will also begin to yearn for a priest to preside pastorally among the nascent congregation, not only in their daily life and ministry but liturgically as well, manifesting the welcoming, hosting aspect of the congregation in relation to the neighborhood. This is likely to require full-time engagement in a variety of areas. Already, however, even without a priest, something crucial has taken place: the members of the group understand themselves as biblical interpreters and *doers* of ministry, an identity perhaps not articulated in theological language, but lived out through weekly practice.

Stage 2: Choosing a priest
As the weeks go by this fledgling community is beginning to feel that they need an ordained person to pastorally preside among them. I reiterate that the members are not going to be ministered *to* by a priest, but rather they are already discovering *their* call and witness as Christian ministers—the word means servants—particularly to those in need. Their gathering is, quite literally, the first fruits of the reign of God appearing in their neighborhood.

They deserve the best clergy that the bishop can find for them, and therefore the search for their ordained leadership should be a national one, and not limited to the local diocese—particularly since most dioceses have precious few Latino clergy to choose from. It would be ideal for this fledging community to discern a vocation to priesthood in one or more of its members, but that may be possible only after a couple of years.

The ideal priest will be Latino, preferably with some ability in English language and American culture, but not necessarily. Better to hire a talented priest who speaks mostly Spanish than a bilingual priest with no pastoral or cultural skills. Sometimes it is necessary for Anglo priests with some bilingual ability to step up to the plate. In those cases, their ministry will be more effective if they understand themselves to be *learners*, students of a different way of living, rather than as authoritative teachers. I am sorry to say that in my experience most Anglo priests cannot make this shift in attitude as long as they insist on thinking that they are bringing something to "improve" Latinos. Additionally, merely knowing a little Spanish and having some familiarity with Latino culture are not enough to preside in a Latino Christian community, any more than speaking English gives someone leadership abilities in an Anglo church.

> The most successful churches have Latino/Hispanic clergy, . . . offer services in Spanish, . . . have their own building or installation, and a . . . dominant Latino/Hispanic congregation—even if it operates as a mission or parallel to the dominant Anglo Sunday congregation. This finding is corroborated in the Pew Religion Study.
> —*Creating a Welcoming Presence*

The ideal priest will also be experienced in Christian formation (as outlined, for example, in the next chapter and in Appendix A). Additionally, some experience in training Latinos—especially lay leaders in the process of becoming Anglicans (as outlined in Appendix B)—would also be extremely helpful, for the priest's primary task for the foreseeable future will be to form Anglican Christian members and leaders, equipping them for their ministries to the neighborhood.

If possible, the priest should be trained in the United States, in a Master of Divinity seminary program with a specialization in Latino ministry. In order to serve as priest, a church founder must have not only compassion and empathy, but also a deep theological understanding of what a Christian community is called to be. The fledgling priest must grapple with questions such as, "What is the core of Jesus' preaching?" "How did his message and witness get him into trouble? Why?" "What is the relationship between 'the church' as a gathered assembly and 'the good news of Jesus'?" "What is the relationship between the Christian assembly and the Reign of God?" Without this understanding it is all too easy to fall to the temptations of cultural deviations of the church, such as clericalism, commercialism, or careerism.

The priest must also be fully conversant in the polity and governance of the Episcopal Church. In the anecdote above, Father Jorge, a former Roman Catholic, had not spent much time practicing the differences in polity between the Roman and Episcopal churches. This created a high level of frustration, both on his side and the bishop's.

The priest should be called under a contract with the diocese expiring in five years but renewable for another five, making the mutual expectations of the diocese and the priest clear, and paving a way to redeploy the priest if he or she fails to meet them. It goes without saying, however, that both sides must have a role in determining these expectations. Without clarity about the specific goals expected of the priest, all of the parties involved will simply do whatever comes naturally to them, whether adequately Episcopal or not.

Stage 3: Developing a fledgling assembly

Now that we have a fledging group of leaders gathering for Bible reflection on a regular basis at a given location and a priest called to preside among them, the first thing the new priest needs to do is to join and observe the Bible reflection group. Note that I say *observe*, not *lead*. This is extremely difficult for Latino clergy to do, for we have a hierarchical conception of the church—clergy and laity alike—and as soon as a priest steps into a group of laity all opinions cease and all eyes and ears are turned to him or her. The priest must consciously fight this tendency, returning to the lay members their projected authority rather than dressing up in it herself. She should "visit" the group, thanking them for coming together, assuring them of her support and availability, passing the reins to the lay leader of the group, then leaving to do something else—or, if she stays, actively *listening* to what the members are expressing. The priest is not in the group to teach, judge, or set things right. These are important activities, but they will take place in different venues.

Stage 4: Articulating the assembly's mission and goals

Soon after the priest's arrival the leadership of the fledgling assembly should begin to plan a retreat with the goal of articulating a vision of the work of the new community. This is to be the *community*'s vision. The priest, if at all professional, will know the difference between his vision and the community's, holding back when needed on his own sense of where they should go in order to foster their own vision and responsibility for it. But the priest must also be careful: "I do not know what we should do" is not an acceptable statement in Latino culture for powerful persons to make. Instead, it is much better for the priest to say, "I think we should try to express what each of us feels called to do as individuals and as a group to witness to God's love in this neighborhood." Through statements such as these the priest is embracing the responsibility to lead while keeping the goal of their shared journey open.

The group will be tempted to express vague, pious feelings, staying as abstract as possible. "We want to be a welcoming, loving community" is a fine sentiment, but it can hardly be a tool for assessing progress. Rather, the retreat should encourage the participants to name concrete goals for the new congregation:

Over the next year, we will:

- ❦ increase membership by 20 percent;
- ❦ develop a ministry to hospitalized people;
- ❦ develop immigration counseling and referral services.

The same type of visioning process may lead to a five-year plan marked by clear milestones along the way. For example, the new assembly may decide to try to meet its budget by an additional 10 percent each year until by the sixth year the members are responsible for 50 percent of the expenses.

Finally, as we saw in our opening story, three years was not enough time to support and sustain a nascent Latino congregation. Support for at least five, and preferably ten years should be planned by the diocese. In Father Jorge's case, the diocese pulled financial support much too early, without warning, creating a crisis for both priest and congregation. Suddenly the church doors were closed. Yet behind the scenes, it turns out that Father Jorge made some political mistakes in the diocese, and closing the parish under the guise of financial concerns was a way for a conflict-averse bishop to fire him. The fifty souls he left behind apparently did not matter to her. Needless to say, Latinos find this kind of episcopal cowardice scandalous, for we expect those who wield power to do so openly and without embarrassment.

Stage 5: Forming the natural leaders as Christians
The new priest is in place and wants to teach the fledgling assembly—understanding, however dimly, that part of her call is precisely to teach. So she starts an inquirers' class that is open to all, and begins by showing them the movie *Elizabeth*. Underneath her decision is the assumption that she has the knowledge that will "answer" the questions she thinks her "students" should be asking. She does have a certain knowledge of the Christian faith, of course, but she hardly knows what existential questions will arise from the members' life experiences.

The main teaching ministry of a priest is *not* to teach the history of Anglicanism, but to teach the Good News of Jesus, and what difference this gospel can make in the congregation's life and the world beyond it. The development of an Anglican identity must be founded on Christian maturity. The latter is essential to the former. Without it we will have congregations with exquisite Anglican worship where people hate each other.

In sum, the priest must encourage and support a proactive, conscious process of Christian formation, in a group setting and not only individually. Worship and

31

preaching, of course, are formative events, but in both cases the congregation is rather passive, belying their call to be active ministers of the gospel.

[One of the obstacles to Latino ministry in the Episcopal Church is that] there is no program for the creation of leadership and lay leadership; one that recognizes how our leadership is currently created and where glass ceilings need to be lifted to foster true change. It also seems that all denominations are struggling with the issue of leadership and the creation of lay leadership. Most of their plans focus on this shortfall but lack "how to" details or an examination of subgroups within Latino/Hispanic target groups. —*Creating a Welcoming Presence*

The next chapter engages a process of active formation in groups (outlined in Appendix A), and presents tools for developing the four main proficiencies of the Christian life: Bible interpretation, active worship, a rich prayer life, and committed service. These are developed through participation in a group "safe space" where the fledgling members can explore the meaning of being a Christian *for them* as Latinos, which is probably different from its meaning to Augustine or Thomas Aquinas or Queen Elizabeth.

Participants in this group will spend the better part of a year exploring their lives in the light of the Scriptures. As their turning toward specifically Christian behaviors grows and develops, they will be supported by sponsors and the rest of the group, becoming increasingly conscious and able to name their growth in the Christian life. This may lead them to Christian initiation or, if already baptized, to reaffirming their commitment through confirmation or reception into the Episcopal Church, as they reaffirm the covenant made at their baptism. This style of Christian formation—biblically centered, grounded in the creation of a "safe space" where all are encouraged to share their experience in the light of Scripture—is helpful for all church planting ventures, but particularly so for Latinos. For one thing, as we will see below, relationships are at the core of how we see the world, and thus we naturally prefer to reflect with a group of friends than alone with a book. Additionally, the experience of being encouraged to voice one's personal sense of how the text relates to daily life is a profound experience for participants who tend to believe that the only one with a theological voice is the priest.

I cannot overemphasize the importance of this group. Without such a clear, proactive, deeply committed way of welcoming members to a Christian assembly, new church members often remain chronically marginalized, unclear about the gospel, and therefore prey to superstitious understandings of the Christian religion.

Once this process of formation is well under way, perhaps as much as a full year after arrival, the priest will need to develop a different group for a different sort of persons: "Becoming Anglicans" (or a more felicitous title) is a coordinated series of discussions, led by the priest, to acquaint committed members with various central aspects of Anglican history and theology and specifically Episcopal governance at the congregational, diocesan, national, and global levels. (Appendix B presents an outline of such a program.)

Over forty years' history of ministry with Latino/Hispanic communities provides us with an awareness of what works and what does not work. This period of ministry, often a result of trial and error, has resulted in an awareness of the ingredients necessary for effective ministry in Latino communities.

—*Creating a Welcoming Presence*

Both of these formation groups—the Bible reflection group and "Becoming Anglicans"—are essential to developing a mature congregation: the first because, as Tertullian said, Christians are *made,* not born; the second, because even many lifelong Episcopalians do not know the differences among Anglicanism, Roman Catholicism, and mainline Protestantism, let alone how the local congregation is governed. Additionally, the second group is very helpful in empowering lay leaders. Usually at least 20 percent of a congregation's members wish to exercise leadership functions of some kind, from serving on the vestry to assisting in worship, teaching, and taking care of the building. An important part of any priest's ministry is to identify, support, and empower lay leaders.

THE "NESTED" CONGREGATION

The formerly African-American urban congregation in South Chicago now prides itself on being a multicultural parish. Latinos, Chinese, and Caribbean blacks all worship in the same church, although they have a tendency to attend the worship service most comfortable to each ethnic group. One weekday evening, as I waited for the members of the vestry to arrive for a special meeting, I went into the kitchen to look for milk for my coffee. I opened the refrigerator and found three quarts of milk. One was labeled "Hispanic Milk," another "Caribbean Milk," and a third "Chinese Milk."

I was not surprised later to find out that the church has three budgets: the "regular" congregation's budget, the Chinese congregation's budget, and the Latino congregation's budget. The church's endowment is used to finance the salary and benefits for the rector, who is African American. Funding for the Chinese and Latino congregations and their needs is cobbled together from different sources.

Before we turn to the steps needed to establish a "nested" congregation, I must confess that in my experience it is often preferable, when at all possible, to develop a new Latino congregation "from scratch." The reasons for this preference are many, but most of them relate to the inability of members of any dominant culture to trust people who are different from themselves. This chronic state of distrust and fighting for control leads to deep and lasting divisions that are difficult to overcome, as the story of the "three milks" illustrates, making it difficult for a Latino congregation to grow and flourish.

One of the problems in the past was that Latino/Hispanic ministry development initiatives in the Episcopal Church focused on broad demographics and lacked clear, immediate, actionable, and measurable goals for evaluation of progress and did not allow for ongoing adjustments. —*Creating a Welcoming Presence*

"My (Anglo) vestry won't let me" is a refrain heard from clergy in these situations more often than it should. Dedicated and hard-working though he was, Father Jorge had no idea how to deal with his threatened vestry, most of whom saw the development of a Latino congregation in their midst as a sign of their failure to lead their church into a secure financial position. In that case, the time and energy necessarily spent on pastoring a dying congregation and their fearful attempts to control outcomes could have been much better spent nurturing a new assembly of Latinos.

Nevertheless, we need models for developing a "nested" Latino congregation, since sometimes there is no other choice. But I offer this model with a word of warning to priests who are considering such a step: *Don't try this by yourselves!* You will need the support of your bishop and the expertise of the diocesan Latino ministries coordinator. Take your time, be ready to learn from mistakes, and remember that it is not *your* church. It will also help immensely if you are able to see the development of a nested Latino congregation as a step toward your being eventually replaced as rector by a bilingual, bicultural Latino. And if you are an Anglo vicar in charge of a mission with only a few members, please do not attempt this. Your congregation is too weak to stand the stresses that a new Latino congregation in their midst will cause.

Step 1: Consider your location
If you are thinking of "nesting" a Latino congregation I assume that your parish is located in a heavily Latino neighborhood—otherwise, why try this? Ideally, the diocese will have earmarked several large churches in heavily Latino neighborhoods that are either in danger of closing due to attrition or are undergoing a transition to new clergy leadership in the next five to ten years, whether through retirement or relocation, and your parish is one of these.

Step 2: Create a development strategy
Perhaps you are lucky enough to work in a diocese with a canon law that allows the bishop to close a parish if its membership reaches below a certain level. I know of one such case in which the bishop was not afraid to intervene. Noticing that the fifteen remaining Anglo congregants were not allowing any of the fifty or so Latinos in regular attendance to become official members, let alone elect them to the vestry, the bishop used his prerogative to close the parish and reopen it a few years later as a Latino mission. In some situations it is better to close an "old" congregation or merge its congregants with an existing

neighboring one, and then reopen the church facilities as a full Latino congregation and develop it from scratch.

In any case, once you have considered all the options, propose to the vestry the development of a Latino congregation in your church, noting the bishop's encouragement. Make sure they do not think that their problems will be solved through this. The development of a Latino congregation cannot save a dwindling congregation from closing, let alone resolve its financial troubles. This should not be a step taken to remedy financial distress or to "give new life" to the dying Anglo congregation. Bring a development strategy to the vestry and be ready to modify it in response to their suggestions, but do not succumb to delay tactics.

Step 3: Fund a budget
Plan in hand, go to the Diocesan Council with a request for funding for the coming five years, beginning with full funding and decreasing by 10 percent each year. Expect to extend assistance for another five years if necessary, but continue decreasing it toward zero at the end of the tenth year.

Step 4: Identify Latino leaders
Through a series of neighborhood explorations, as described above, find and identify Latino leaders of the neighborhood. Besides these, gather and commission a group of volunteer Latino "missionaries" from other churches—Episcopal or not—to help develop this new congregation. Make sure they can identify and encourage potential lay leaders in the neighborhood, sharing

their expertise with these new leaders but returning to their parishes of origin after no more than a year.

Step 5: Call a priest

Do a national search for a priest who would fill a full-time position in the nested congregation. The ideal candidate would be a bilingual Latino priest with a Master of Divinity degree. Interview broadly and get feedback from the lay Latino missionaries and from Latino leaders throughout the diocese, particularly if you are a monolingual Anglo bishop or rector, as your discernment and interviewing skills will be severely compromised.

Develop a contract with the priest for five years. If there is a chance that the rector of the parish might leave or retire soon, make sure the Latino priest has the right to run for that position when the time comes. Resist the temptation to have two separate congregations with two separate rectors and budgets. Insist on one parish with one budget, one rector, one assisting priest, and two services, one in English and one in Spanish. After all, we all drink the same milk—spiritual *and* bovine.

The contract should also specify clear patterns and periods of supervision by the diocese and an annual evaluation of the new congregation's growth in welcoming newcomers, forming them as Christians and Anglicans, developing increasing service to the neighborhood, and economic self-sufficiency. Make financial self-sufficiency a clear goal, to be achieved over a period of five to ten years.

Step 6: Plan for growth
Ask the fledging Latino congregation and its priest to attend a retreat with you or a facilitator to develop a growth plan for Latino ministry in your parish. Name achievable goals, and make sure they are measurable.

Step 7: Evaluate growth regularly
Evaluate the performance of the Latino priest regularly, and, starting after the third year, begin assessing whether the priest can in fact take the congregation to a place of meeting its budget halfway by the sixth year. Be ready and willing to redeploy the priest at the end of the fifth year if it looks like the congregation will not be self-sufficient in another five years. Ten years is plenty of time.

Carefully monitor from the start whether the Latino priest is delegating authority to emerging lay leaders. Without delegation, he or she will tend to do everything and eventually the congregation will level off at about sixty members, an unrealistically small size if they are ever going to be self-sufficient.

Step 8: Encourage diocesan support
The bishop and diocesan Latino ministry coordinator should stay in close touch with the Latino priest, the Latino lay leaders, the rector, and the vestry. Latinos *expect* episcopal and diocesan oversight, and are nonplussed when bishops act as if they have no clear expectations of the members of their dioceses. Latinos will want the bishop to expect monthly financial and ministerial reports, and to take a personal interest at key points of Christian formation programs. Consider host-

ing a Lenten retreat with the bishop, for example, that is open to all in the Bible reflection group.

Twice a year the bishop or a diocesan official in charge of Latino ministry (preferably Latino) should chair a meeting of the vestry and the leaders of the Latino ministry to examine progress made in terms of:

- percentage of newcomers becoming members;
- Christian formation of members;
- ongoing lay leadership training;
- relationship between Sunday attendance and becoming a member;
- percentage of members pledging;
- gospel witness of the congregation in the neighborhood.

These are only a few suggestions for how Latino congregations can be started from scratch or nested in an existing congregation. Much more could be said, of course, but at its core, the development of Latino congregations will not succeed in the long term if they are:

- expected to "rescue" dying Anglo congregations.
- understood as Spanish versions of Anglo ministry, ignoring cultural differences.

❦ led by clergy who are left to drift by their bishops and diocesan staffs, without naming expectations or establishing clear goals and holding regular evaluations.

❦ placed in a chronically dependent relationship to the diocese, without the expectation of ever reaching financial self-sufficiency.

❦ developed as a sacramental "store" without enough energy and funds spent on the formation of Christian and Episcopal members and lay leaders.

❦ unable to generate and raise up future clergy and lay leaders from their midst.

The prospect of generating a Latino assembly of members of Christ's body can be an exciting process, but it can also be a soul-killing experience for all concerned. A certain amount of proactive realism is necessary, honoring cultural diversity, humbly going where God is calling and being patient but determined and clear about the expectations and responsibilities of all concerned.

CHAPTER 3

Forming Latino Christians

Many Anglo church leaders assume that all Latinos in the United States are Roman Catholic. And in fact, if you stopped a number of Latinos on the street and asked them, they would probably agree. But if you also asked them when was the last time they attended a church, they would be likely to scratch their heads. "My cousin's wedding, maybe five years ago?" they would wonder.

Many Latinos assume they are Roman Catholic because they were baptized so. They often do not know of any other alternative. "Catholic" is what most respectable people in Latin America say they are, and others follow suit. But the fact is that the great majority of Latinos reaching our shores are *underchurched*. They were baptized as infants, perhaps made their first communion after a hasty drilling by a parish priest, and have seldom attended church since.

Most inquirers' programs in the Episcopal Church, where they exist at all, are concerned with making sure the participants understand the difference between Roman Catholicism and Anglicanism, and the history of Anglican worship and church polity. These are surely laudable goals, but they are premature, for many Latinos lack the most basic proficiencies of Christian living. Like the other unchurched people that make up a considerable portion of American society today, few Latinos have developed an ability to participate actively and consciously in worship. We lack the most basic Bible literacy and do not know how to go about nourishing a life of prayer. Few of us have developed a habit of service on behalf of the poor and marginalized.

Build programs that create spiritual growth and increase self-esteem:
• Offer programs that will nourish the faith journey at their own speed and style.
• Offer prayer groups, retreats, groups on parenting, finding your inner self, Bible Study, etc.
• Offer leadership conferences and lay leadership training.
—*Creating a Welcoming Presence*

Any serious attempt to improve the Christian formation of Latinos must begin with these four areas, particularly with their evangelization, for the truth is, in many cases they have not yet heard the gospel of Jesus Christ.

As they practice these four areas of development, new Latino members will begin asking searching questions about contradictions with their cultural assumptions: "Is it really true that the priest is *married*?" "What do you mean this is *not* a Catholic church?" And so on. These questions are important, for they present "teachable moments" about Anglican or Episcopal identity. But they do not lie at the core of *Christian* identity.

In the third century Tertullian wrote that "Christians are made, not born." Many may find this slightly scandalous, assuming that being a Christian is no different from being a good human being. But being a Christian is more than that. It involves developing abilities such as forgiving one's enemies, looking out for the underprivileged, and witnessing with all one's life and substance to the gospel of Christ. These are not "natural" human behaviors. They are behaviors learned in the context of a supportive Christian family and congregation.

This process of developing "Christian expertise" was understood by the early church as a process of introducing a person not to a set of doctrines, but into a different way of living. Formation implied a radical turning around (*metanoia*) and learning new habits. The process took place along four different but complementary axes of development:

1. The ability to interpret the biblical text and make it one's own.

2. The ability to engage in corporate worship in an active, conscious way.

3. The ability to pray.

4. The ability to minister to (serve) the poor and outcast, in witness to the gospel.

If we are to have mature Latino Christians in the church today we will have to take this fourfold process of becoming Christian seriously and develop ways to support it. (See Appendix A for an outline of such a program.) The following sections describe the salient features of this process of formation in the lives of Latinos today, the first of which is developing the ability to engage the Bible.

Latinos Interpret the Bible

We all shared what phrase or aspect of the story of the crossing of the Red Sea that stayed with us, and Santiago then read the story again, slowly. He was moved when he read the words of God to Moses, "Be still and I will do the fighting," but said nothing about that afterward.

Gloria, the leader, then asked, "I wonder when we have been in situations similar to this?" Herminia put her hand up immediately, dying to share something with the others. "Well, it was the summer of 1978, a terrible year for us. I had just been raped by the Contras in El Salvador. My oldest son had been 'disappeared' and my daughter and husband were murdered before my eyes. I did not know what to do. I was desperate. Then, out of the blue, my sister in Los Angeles called me and told me to come and live with her. At first I was even more afraid to do that than to stay in danger. But I trusted God, hitched a ride to Guatemala with some other widows, and snuck through the Mexican border.

"I worked in Puebla washing dishes in a filthy restaurant for six months, saving all my money to pay a Coyote, the man who would sneak us through the border into California. When the day came, we left at sunset, walking in the dark till we came to a wide river. It was pitch dark and cold, and I did not know where I was going. 'Wait,' I said to the Coyote. 'Let's stop and get used to the darkness.' Then, as I sat there, I saw that the river was very shallow in this part to the left, and we were able to cross into the United States. So you see, in my own life, God has said to me many times, 'Be still and I will do the fighting.'"

Afterward, beaming with amazement, she came to me and said, "Juan! I thought I was going to be told what to believe, but I found that my views were respected even when other people who were better educated than I did not agree! I feel like I can say anything in this group!" Herminia had found her theological voice.

The almost total lack of Christian formation in our Latino congregations often results in a community of people who are seriously underdeveloped spiritually. Their divine call to be mature, active members of Christ's assembly sent into the world to serve has long been disregarded by well-meaning but uninformed church leaders. Latino Christians who have fallen into superstitious and magical understandings of religion and who have an underdeveloped awareness regarding their own systematic oppression and abuse have not been challenged with clear expectations regarding membership in the church, let

47

alone provided with the means of growing in that membership.

Learning to understand our lives in the light of Scripture requires commitment and patience, but above all it requires respect for our theological voices, the voices that can use biblical metaphors to tell the wonderful things God has done for us. Above all, true biblical literacy requires from us, as leaders, awe and respect for the mystery of God's calling "the least of these" to speak that divine wisdom to us. Without this foundational respect for those whom God has called, we can hardly nurture and support *their ways* of participating actively in worship, growing in prayer, and committing to service.

LATINOS WORSHIP

My friend Helen and I were on a trip to Chiapas. Sunday came and we decided to go to the main church in town—Roman Catholic, as there were no Episcopal churches there. We arrived early for the locals, even though we were right on time by our watches. A few women were placing vases full of water around the main altar and throughout the chancel. Some candles flickered already in front of statues of saints.

Eventually the service started, even though the church was only half-full. As more people began to arrive, we saw that many of them had stopped outside the church to buy bunches of flowers, and were now carrying them directly to the ready vases, where they dropped and arranged them—rather cursorily, I thought.

The priest spoke loudly, close to his microphone, and clearly thought he was a one-man show. Now and then there was some rather dispirited singing. The congregation seemed passive, but at the same time we noticed some families were doing things Helen had never seen before. At the church steps one family lighted candles and stuck them on the floor right in the middle of the entrance, so people had to walk around them. They sprinkled rose petals among the candles, which were four different colors—three of each color. The colors seemed to have some specified meaning, as did the order in which they were placed.

The family then went inside the church, stopping first to deposit some coins in the hat of the leader of the St. Thomas' fraternity; evidently they have a special relationship with that saint, I surmised. They found a pew and sat distractedly through the first reading. Then the grandmother gathered her bundle and approached a rather bloody statue of Jesus at the flagellation. She opened her bundle, took out more candles, and lighted them, placing them firmly on the statue's base. She then addressed Jesus in broken Spanish, as her native language was a Mayan dialect. When she finished, she pulled a coin out of her pocket and placed it with a loud "thwack" on the base.

Relatively few people received communion, even though by then the church was packed. The service over, some people left, while other families lit candles and sprinkled rose petals. We noticed about fifteen women, their heads covered with shawls, going up to the reredos behind the altar. They knelt in the chancel, right up next to the tabernacle—as close as they could get to Jesus. They pulled out their rosaries and began reciting the prayers; the one who was obviously the leader knew exactly what pleading tone of voice to use to get the rest weeping profusely. It was heartbreaking, and we felt like we had entered into a completely foreign, ancient space.

Throughout the service Helen wondered what was happening. She found it difficult to follow the liturgy, not only because her Spanish is very rusty, but because all the activity around her made it hard to concentrate. The priest's body language, the choir members' alternatively distracted and attentive presence, the children coming and going, the candle lighting and praying out loud—all felt very foreign to her. Helen said to me, "There is so much stuff in this kind of worship!" She felt disconnected and fascinated at the same time.

If we were to take a woman of Chiapas to a Latino Episcopal Church in the United States she would be as nonplussed by the service as Helen was. The priest's informality would shock her. She might feel disappointed that there was no place ready to accept the fresh flowers she had brought: there are only two tiny vases of flowers on the reredos behind the altar. She will find no place to do her ancient devotions—indeed, there may be only one small statue in a corner and since it is made of white marble she cannot figure out who it is. No one is lighting candles or talking to God out loud, let alone talking to the saints. It would be hard for her to believe this is a real church—it feels rather like a classroom, especially when the priest reads the sermon from the pulpit. "If the priest needs to read it, he doesn't know what he is talking about!" a Latino once told me.

When will we develop a truly Latino Episcopal liturgy? What we have now in the United States and much of Anglican Latin America is an Anglo liturgy in Spanish. Instead, Episcopal (or Methodist, Presbyterian, Lutheran) Latino worship must go to its Latin American roots to recover its soul, for the elements of our liturgical practice are quite different from those of the dominant culture.

Latino Worship	Anglo Worship
Time is flexible, elastic.	Time is evenly measured.
Participate through things: flowers, candles, and offerings.	Participate through listening: singing, and offering money.
Visual images are important.	Visual images are secondary.
Emotional preaching.	Intellectual preaching.
The sermon is extemporaneous.	The sermon is read from a text.
Chant or popular music.	"Classical" hymnody or folk music.
Engages the physical.	Engages ideas.
Sense of being at a fiesta or a fair.	Sense of being in a lecture hall.

These differences provoke many questions:

- ❧ What is the essence of Anglican worship?

- ❧ How can we incarnate Anglican liturgy in our Latino culture?

- ❧ Can we create a truly Latino worship and remain Anglican?

The historical answer to the last question is *yes*. Anglican and Roman Catholic liturgies have common roots in the early and medieval church, so there are many elements that they share. Anglicanism has a broad spectrum of worship traditions and ways of praying, from simple to elaborate, from Protestant to Catholic, from private to corporate. Latino worship often does incorporate more Roman Catholic elements than some Anglicans, especially those from the "low church" tradition, appreciate or feel comfortable doing. When people say that Latino worship "is not Anglican," they often really mean, "We don't like that way of worshiping," or perhaps, "That is not Anglo."

Strengths of the Episcopal Church
in relation to Latino worship:
• Engaging music with strong integration,
participation, and volunteer choir
• Meaningful sermons
• Familiar liturgy
• Lay ministry opportunities
• Focus on spiritual formation
• Christian education for children
• Social service programs
• Hospitality
• Special celebrations: Virgen de Guadalupe,
Quinceañeras, and Día de los Muertos.
—*Creating a Welcoming Presence*

What then is *Anglican* liturgy? It cannot merely be English liturgy colonizing the whole world, for then we could hardly call ourselves a universal (catholic) church. We may have exported English worship in the eighteenth century and called it Anglican worship, but that time has passed. If Anglicanism is going to claim that it is a catholic church it must welcome a worldwide array of different styles of worship arising from a worldwide array of cultures. Still, we must do so while honoring several essential aspects of historic Anglican worship even as we experience it in a Latino context.

Anglican liturgy is vernacular
One of the glories of Anglicanism is its *Book of Common Prayer*, which was first compiled by Thomas Cranmer in 1549. Along with other continental reformers, Cranmer insisted that the church's worship had to be in the language of the people. He understood that liturgy is, before anything else, a communication event, and the words being communicated in the prayers and Scripture readings of the liturgy must be understood by the people.

Human communication, however, takes place in the context of a given language and culture. Communication cannot be separated from culture and language, which means that as a communicative event, worship must be inculturated: it must be incarnated in the language, customs, and "ways of doing things" of a specific people. Only then can our worship witness to the gospel of Jesus Christ effectively. Perhaps this is why so many Latinos in the United States prefer to worship in Latino churches, in Spanish, led by Latino clergy.

Cranmer and the reformers also knew that communication does not take place only through language: we can also gain understanding visually, audibly, and kinetically.

Thus the sights and sound of worship and the ways we move (or not) in the ritual space also constitute a form of communication. The first *Book of Common Prayer* and all its subsequent revisions allow for flexibility and breadth of expression in these nonverbal ways of worshiping, and it is in these expressions that we see such a variety today, from Anglicans dancing up the aisle to receive communion in a church in Uganda to New Guineans incorporating hula dances in the proclamation of the gospel.

The presupposition for liturgy that is transformative of both personal and societal living is that it be imaginative and engaging. But for it to be that it must be inculturated, for only an inculturated liturgy can have witness value.
—James Empereur and Eduardo Fernández, *La Vida Sacra: Contemporary Hispanic Sacramental Theology*

Anglican liturgy is biblical

The Anglican Church was born in the Reformation and it shares with other Reformation churches, and with the Roman Catholic Church after Vatican II, a focus on the Bible in its liturgies. Not only do Anglicans give a central place to the proclamation of God's word within every ritual event, but we also craft many of our prayers using biblical imagery and phrases.

Anglican liturgy is incarnational

The many liturgical traditions within Anglicanism span a wide range of sensory expressions, from vestments, candles, chanting, and incense to silence and simplicity in worship. This diversity serves well a Latino culture that treasures symbolic expression through sensual means. Additionally, the Oxford Movement's gift of grounding the liturgy and social justice in the mystery of the Incarnation makes Anglican liturgy more accessible to Latinos, who worship God as an incarnated presence more easily than as an intellectual concept.

"...the world is a sacrament of God."
—Leonardo Boff, *The Sacraments of Life and the Life of the Sacraments*

Anglican liturgy is syncretic

Anglicanism has a long history of borrowing, integrating, and putting together liturgical elements from all over the world and throughout the ages, from Jewish, Roman, and Greek sources to seventh-century Mozarabic Spanish prayers to more recently composed prayers and liturgies from the Roman Catholic and Protestant liturgical renewal movements. When we are tempted to say a particular prayer or practice is "not Anglican," we need to ask ourselves what we mean by "Anglican." Chances are some Anglicans somewhere along the way have already done it that way before.

Anglican liturgy expresses diversity in unity
Finally, Anglican liturgy is Trinitarian, not only because, like the liturgies of the early church, we offer worship to the Father through the Son in the Holy Spirit, but because our liturgies celebrate unity in diversity. They celebrate our unity as one body in and through our cultural diversity of languages and liturgical practices, as well as the unity of the local assembly through a diversity of complementary liturgical roles. There is no such thing as a private Anglican liturgy.

LATINO PRAYER AND SPIRITUALITY

The vestry members from a Latino congregation in northern California were meeting for a retreat at a larger parish in the suburbs. Its chapel was a beautiful Craftsman-style building, built all in redwood in the early twentieth century. As we wrapped up our retreat I encountered the junior warden, who was walking around the building, staring at the redwood. "Father," he said, "I thought you said this was a well-off congregation."

"Yes, it is," I replied.

"Well, it doesn't look like they can afford any paint!" he countered. "This place is so sad!"

"How would you change it?"

"Well, for one thing, I'd get some color in here, and some flowers and candles, and definitely some statues of saints. What is a church without its saints?"

Like Anglican liturgy, Latino prayer is tangible, visible, and audible. Many Latinos will assume that to relate to God one is *assisted* rather than deterred by objects such as statues, holy cards, rosaries, flowers, candles, and incense. Latino spirituality does not aspire to relate to the divine directly, without sensory mediations. In this sense at least, Latino spirituality is fundamentally sacramental as it employs signs and symbols as mediators and facilitators of the encounter with God.

Some people have a hard time understanding this, and lean toward the more Protestant tendency of considering all such mediations "idolatrous." But during a recent visit to Latin America an elderly indigenous woman taught me a lesson. Let me tell you the story of the old Indian and the statue.

My friend and I entered a dark church in a small village in southern Mexico. We sat down toward the back and observed what was going on. Several people were lighting candles in front of statues of saints, and others brought flowers and deposited them in vases laid out for that purpose. Near us, I spotted a diminutive elderly woman, barefoot, dirty, and dressed practically in rags. She carried a bundle tied up in her *rebozo* (shawl). She approached a statue of the virgin, opened up her bundle, took out about a dozen candles, lit them, and stuck them with hot wax on the edge of the statue's base. She then took out some flowers, tore up the petals, and sprinkled them around the burning candles. Taking a step back, she looked intently at the statue of the Virgin Mary, and then started to pray.

"Most sacred, purest Mother of God, mother of all the human race, you worried over your Son when he was lost in the Temple, and you suffered with him at the foot of the cross. You understand the suffering of all mothers. Have mercy on my son, who is in Los Angeles without a job. Protect him as you protected your own Son and keep him from danger. Please intercede with your Father, and your Son, to bless and protect him in this time of danger for him. . . . "

She went on for some time in long, complex sentences with a certain baroque flavor. As she turned to leave our eyes met, and I followed her out of the church.

"Señora," I said, "excuse me, but I am not from here and I could not help but hear your prayers to the Virgin."

Shyly, she said, "Yes, my son is going through a very difficult time."

"I was wondering," I pushed on, "how is it that the statue of the Virgin, made of wood, hears you?"

The woman stared at me in utter disbelief. "Señor! The statue does not hear me! The *Virgin* does!"

"But where is the Virgin, if not here in the statue?"

"In *heaven*, of course."

"So you could pray to her directly, anywhere, like in your home?" I inquired.

"Yes, of course, but I like to have a reminder of her in front of me when I talk to her." And she walked off in utter wonder at the stupidity of this intellectual who did not understand about prayer.

Latino spirituality is incarnational
Latinos have a much greater sophistication and ability to engage meaningfulness of physical things than we are

given credit for. The fact that we are good at reading the symbolic meaning of the physical world does not mean, however, that we necessarily take symbols *literally*. Rather, like a good theatergoer, we engage metaphors and signs with a "willing suspension of disbelief," as Coleridge would say. We willingly enter into their meaningfulness, just as the theatergoer willingly forgets that she is watching an actor and enters into King Lear's deep sorrow and madness. Furthermore, we seem to be able in our Latino humanity to find meaning—even divine meaning—in everything and anything around us.

Latino spirituality is communal rather than individual
Latinos understand ourselves not only as individuals but principally as members of a large network. I am not simply Juan Oliver, but also Juan and Awilda's first son; the brother of José, Awilda, Joaquin, Carmen, and Teresa; the uncle of their children, too numerous to name here; and John's partner and therefore related to his sister and brothers, uncles and nieces, and so on.

> I am a particular, concrete, and unique embodiment of all those relationships, when someone encounters me they also encounter my parents, relatives, friends, community, my people, as well as the God who created me and the earth that nourishes me.
> —Roberto Goizueta, *Caminemos con Jesús*

Thus it is a little strange for Latinos to be told that we are self-made individuals, when we patently are not. Like it or not, unless I have broken relationships with my extended family, "my spirituality" is "our spirituality," allowing this "us" to extend far beyond family, town, and even nation.

Latino spirituality is popular, rather than elitist
Latinos are fed and supported spiritually by a wide array of popular religious expressions: pilgrimages, novenas, processions, community celebrations, and fairs. We find it difficult to separate what is strictly secular from what is strictly religious.

At bottom what is celebrated [in the fiesta]
is life as gift, and the fiesta is the liturgical act
whereby the community receives and responds
to the gift.... The fiesta—whether expressly civil
or religious—is a fundamentally religious act.
—Roberto Goizueta, *Caminemos con Jesús*

Many of these practices have ancient roots and are not always directly related to the church's hierarchical ministry, but they often are essential aspects of a Latino person's spiritual life.

LATINO SERVICE TO THE POOR

Filiberto Novato, an elderly gentleman from Mexico, was the de facto leader of our small Latino congregation in the South Bronx. He had been a colonizer in Chiapas, sent there by the Mexican government to develop new towns. His leadership was profound, and utterly natural.

One Sunday, during the prayers of the people, which by that time we were offering extemporaneously, he prayed for "Martin, my neighbor, who is very sick with cancer." After the Eucharist, someone asked him during the coffee hour who was this Martin. It turned out that he was known by some of the members of the congregation. As coffee hour was winding down, Filiberto said, "Folks, why don't we make a visit to Martin and bring him some food. I'm sure he can use it." About twelve people from the parish then packed up six or seven bags of food from the pantry and walked over to Martin's house. This was nothing unusual for them—caring for their neighbors is entirely natural.

For most Latinos poverty and need are daily companions, rather than something exceptional or strange. We all know someone in need: a relative, a friend, the woman down the block. In this context "justice" is not an abstract concept for us, indicating the imposition of secular law, but a term designating a set of rights and obligations as demanded by *God. "No es justo"* means "It isn't fair," not "It isn't legal." We well know from lived experience that there can be unfair laws. Justice, then, for us is the fair treatment of the needy according to God's terms.

The moral claim of the poor

For Latinos the poor, the sick, the jobless, the oppressed, and the abused are not an embarrassment, nor are they living evidence of God's judgment. Latino culture does not embrace the idea that material success, good health, and human fulfillment are God's reward for living virtuous lives, nor that the suffering of the poor (understood as a wide category of people in trouble) is evidence of God's judgment visited upon sinners. As a result, Latin Americans do not consider the poor morally suspect; they are "just poor, madam"—unfortunate and in need, and therefore they *have a moral claim on us.* We understand our response to them as a moral obligation, not generosity or charity. For as the fourth-century archbishop Basil the Great so eloquently said, "The shoes in your closet that you do not wear belong to the poor." As a result, insofar as you are known to have means or power, you *must* give and share. To refuse is disgraceful.

Sometimes this generosity reaches the level of heroic, if quiet, virtue. Years ago the Council of Associated Parishes for Liturgy and Mission met in Cuernavaca, Mexico, in order to understand more fully the relationship between the church's worship and service and the wide panoply of cultures in the world. Part of that meeting was spent learning about the realities of the poor in Cuernavaca. We were led to a slum right across the tracks from our conference center; we divided into three groups of ten and were taken by local leaders of the base community there to visit their homes—cardboard shacks randomly arranged along open sewers.

At the end of the day, we all gathered at one of the largest shacks, the home of Luisa, one of the leaders. Sunset was coming and as we usually say evening prayer together, we asked her to lead us in worship. She shyly demurred, explaining that she could not read our Spanish Prayer Book, but we insisted that she tell us a Bible story and lead us in intercessions. She did both perfectly, with the calm authority of an experienced leader. As we finished, she brought out a case of chilled Cokes to offer us. "How did you know we were coming?" I asked incredulously. "Oh, I didn't know. I keep some cold sodas to sell to the kids as they come out of school and this way I have a little extra to help my neighbor who is sick."

The poor as the face of Christ

Although it would be an exaggeration to say that every Latino sees the face of Christ in the poor, it is true that we feel a connection between the poor and God. We glimpse—however dimly—a connection between justice and our own spiritual welfare. This connection may not go beyond a faint sense of responsibility—even guilt—for not attending to the poor, or it may grow to more sophisticated understandings of the interconnections among social and economic structures and the plight of the poor, demanding from us action on a larger scale. The bottom-line, however, is clear. As a friend said to me recently, paraphrasing Matthew 25, "Juan, at the end of time the poor will judge us."

In light of this, we cannot relegate social justice to the role of an addendum to church life under the category of "outreach." The church's life is supposed to be a life of justice-doing, and the indifference of many Christians to the suffering of the world is a scandal.

Build programs to create empowerment opportunities:
• Utilize a series of free counseling and support programs that offer the opportunity to chart a different course in life by making positive changes and advancement as well as acknowledging who [the person]...is today
• Offer training workshops for computer and Internet skills, preparing tax returns, scholarship and college applications, resume writing, and career counseling
• Offer GED training
• Develop a microenterprise program to help those with special talents develop business opportunities
• Offer referral programs for areas of health, finances, law, and education.
—*Creating a Welcoming Presence*

Latinos constantly "do stuff" for people in need. From sending half of their salary to impoverished relatives back home to putting up a jobless friend just evicted from his apartment, Latinos naturally help others, seeing ourselves in their plight. Additionally, we have a strong sense of our interconnections, and often think, "What I do to someone else may come back to me."

Latino generosity is not simply a matter of money. It involves the whole person, giving and receiving of all we have and are. This generosity is built on assumptions of interconnectedness and mutuality. It is not an abstraction. Latinos cannot be generous by just writing a check. If they must do so, they will at least have the decency to deliver it in person, with something more tangible: a small gift, a meal, a hug.

In the same way, Latinos expect the church to be generous, particularly to those in need. In our understanding this is one of the central functions of the church, along with private prayer and corporate worship and the ritualization of life's passages. For Latinos the church is not a corporate project hatched by free individuals with Enlightenment values on a New England green, but a powerful *institution* preceding and outlasting us. Being greater and more powerful than us, it has an obligation to be generous. The worse thing a Latino can say about a local church is not, "They do not help me to grow spiritually there," but, "They do not care about the people in need in this neighborhood; their doors are always closed!" For people in need do not make appointments. We cannot schedule our need.

In sum, for Latinos justice and spirituality cannot be separated. Our saints are a good case in point. You find few pure contemplatives in Latin American hagiography, but there are many friars who defended the rights of Native

Americans against slavery and genocide, monastics who served sick, dying slaves as their ships arrived in Cartagena, and ordinary Christians murdered for siding with the poor against oppressive oligarchies. This long list of saints prevents us from forgetting that holiness is not a nice feeling accomplished by introspection, but largely a matter of acting justly, even unto death.

CHAPTER 4

Forming Latinos in Anglican Polity

Some years ago I took a group of Latinos from our congregation to the diocesan convention. We had earphones and simultaneous interpreters so they could hear and understand everything that was going on. During a break, an elderly woman approached me to ask why some people were at tables while the Latinos were in a separate area. "Oh," I said, "they were elected and we are visitors."

"How does one get elected?" she immediately asked.

"Every parish elects two members to come to convention each year."

"When does that happen?"

"At the annual meeting."

"The what?"

"The annual meeting of the parish."

"What happens there?"

"Well, among other things, the members of the parish elect the vestry and other leaders, and approve the budget."

"Really? I have been on the vestry for ten years and I have never heard of such a thing."

"Well, how did you get on the vestry?"

"Father Rivera appointed me."

"You were not elected by the members?"

"No. Father appoints people who like to help."

"How many are there in your vestry?"

"Five. Let's see, Father Rivera and his wife, the treasurer and his wife, and me."

Apparently neither Father Rivera nor the members of his congregation knew much about Anglican polity and the governance of a congregation. For this reason, once the Christian formation discussed in the previous chapter is well underway, and members of the congregation are consciously and proactively developing their ability to interpret Scripture, participate fully and consciously in worship, lead a life of prayer, and serve the poor, then it is important to focus on what it means to be Anglican. Latino members of the congregation must be Episcopalians who are able to participate in parish life as members equal to our Anglo brothers and sisters in the church. Otherwise, we will always be relegated as second-class members, ignorant of how "things are done" and ultimately unable to live out in community these four areas of Christian expertise.

We sometimes see this marginalization of Latinos in "nested parishes" where the Latino congregation has no representation on the parish board, even though it far outnumbers the English-speaking congregation. It can also be seen in dioceses where there are no Latino delegates to the diocesan convention, let alone the General Convention. To counteract this tendency, Latino clergy must take responsibility, as teachers and pastors in the congregation, to form their members in Anglican ways of governance at all levels, from local to national, as well as in Anglican views of leadership and ministry, stewardship and authority. (Appendix B presents a model for a series of classes covering different aspects of Anglican and Episcopal history, theology, and governance.) Without this grounding in the way we do things in this church, Latinos who are new to the Episcopal Church will be at sea in congregations that govern in ways that seem very strange to them.

But the opposite also needs to be pointed out. Although Latinos must grow into Episcopal and Anglican ways of doing things, the Episcopal Church must also come to understand how Lationos "do" authority and governance. To ignore this is to continue to hold unrealistic expectations of Latinos. We turn now, therefore, to examine Latino ways of governing and exercising authority.

LATINO AUTHORITY AND GOVERNANCE

Some years ago I served as a supply priest on Sundays at a Latino congregation. One Sunday, as I was vesting for the service, the leader of the congregation stepped into the sacristy and asked me, "Father, who is going to read today?"

"I don't know," I replied. "Don't you have a list of people to read, with assigned dates?"

"Oh no!" she said. "That would make them feel like they have to come to church!"

"Well, why don't you see who's here and you decide?"

"Oh, but Father, isn't that what they pay you to do?" she said—rather brazenly, I thought. Then I came to my senses and said, "Joanna, you're right. It's my responsibility as presider of this congregation to delegate the honor of reading the Scriptures to the lay members. So I am delegating it to you, with full confidence that you can choose who should read from now on."

She beamed with pride, and eventually became an excellent coordinator of altar ministries. I never had to choose a reader again.

In this section we will explore Latino expectations of those in power and authority, and how Anglo expectations around the same issues often clash with our cultural assumptions, making the development of Latino ministry more difficult. Even the language we use to define these expectations and assumptions can vary, so we need to start with a few definitions.

First, Latino culture is *hierarchical*. By this I do not mean that it is abusive or patriarchal, as the term is now widely used, but that it understands the world as a system of layered levels of responsibility and power. The more power you have, the more responsibility you have to fulfill what has been entrusted to you and expected of you. It is useless for leaders to claim that they are ordinary people, "just like anyone else," when they patently are *not*. In the liturgy, for example, the vesture, place, postures, and actions of the clergy mark them as *different*: they are ordained persons. I am a priest and Joanna is a parishioner. She cannot be *my* priest and I cannot be *her* parishioner. We are equal in the eyes of God, but we are not interchangeable. Our relationship is not symmetrical.

By *power* I mean the right to tell others what to do, expecting that they will do so. This right (and sometimes duty) is defined by legal instruments such as laws, canons, and church bylaws, and is conferred to a person by virtue of office or title regardless of who one is as an individual.

Authority, by contrast, is a quality of relationships. It must be earned in and through relationships. Insofar as a priest has earned the trust of the parishioners and they are willing to follow his or her lead, the priest has authority with them. Both Anglos and Latinos often confuse power with authority. The difference is that in Latino culture, those who insist on their power without earning their authority are often deeply resented.

Without authority, leaders only have power—the right, legally established, to make others do their will. Latinos will obey people with power, of course, but grumpily. Do not be surprised if they drag their feet and even undermine the pet projects of such leaders. Leaders must earn authority, which means that they must spend time with Latinos; both must learn to trust the other in order for authority to be earned and given.

Additionally, Latinos expect a lot from someone who has power. Although the term is cynically used in English to put down "Lady Bountiful" behaviors that do not take seriously the needs of the poor, *noblesse oblige* actually means, "Nobility obliges me to..."—that is, the fact that I am powerful lays a burden on me to do this. I have to do it precisely because I am powerful. This is not charity. The recipient has a *right* to it.

Latinos share:

• a social/political dynamic regarding group structure and internal organization (i.e., role of leader, type of leadership, internal organization, and group roles)

• a general reliance on extended family and immediate social groups before attempting to affiliate with institutions

• an emphasis on the value of interdependent family relationships rather than on independence

• a respect for elders, professionals, and titles.

—*Creating a Welcoming Presence*

Often non-Latinos in positions of power forget or never learn this aspect of holding power. In Latino culture generosity, even magnanimity, are essential to the exercise of power. If leaders overlook this, they are implying that they are in command simply because they can get away with it—raw power at work, regardless of the contributions, feelings, or needs of others. This is unacceptable and bound to lessen the leader's authority in very short order. Worse, these leaders will be tagged as mean and selfish— people will still obey them, but only outwardly. When leaders are unsure of their authority they may be tempted to overreach with their power, to their peril.

Finally, Latinos respect people in power as long as they act *justly*. By this I certainly do not mean merely legally or canonically, but as God would act, particularly toward the poor and powerless. In the Latino worldview, the distance between the powerful and the powerless is so great (we don't pretend to be all the same) that it must be bridged by the powerful. And so Latinos will be surprised if people in power do *not* command, since it is in fact their job to do so—hopefully after due shared deliberation and dialogue. Disguising one's power under a cloak of false humility will not gain leaders respect with Latinos. Rather, Latinos will assume that the leader is extremely stupid, duplicitous, or lazy in avoiding the responsibility of command. Leaders do not have to pretend to be "Joe Six-packs." Latinos know they are not.

As with carrying a large stick, however, a little power goes a long way. Twenty years ago I was invited to a Latin American diocese to give workshops on welcoming newcomers. Most of the clergy came, about forty of them, some from long distances that required them to stay over two nights at the diocesan center. At lunch, I mentioned to the bishop how honored I was that the clergy had come from so far away. "Oh, they come every month," he said. "Every month?" I dropped my jaw. "Sure," he said. "This is how I do *episcope* (oversight)."

And sure enough, all through the three-hour lunch, among the joking and laughter but never stepping outside his episcopal role, the bishop kept up with his clergy's lives, their projects, successes, and obstacles. He seemed to be socializing, but in fact he was taking the temperature of his diocese in a very sophisticated way, "doing business" while "just socializing." Latinos do not consider it inappropriate to talk business when what brings us together is our work. We are together in these situations in a professional relationship.

LATINO STEWARDSHIP

The bishop's committee was about to deal with the fact that the walls of the chancel badly needed new paint. "I move we form a painting committee to decide the color and raise funds for the project," said the lone Anglo member of the bishop's committee.

"Wait," Lola chimed in, not waiting for the chair to ask for discussion. "Isn't that the job of the junior warden? Shouldn't he get the project together, ask advice, and if we need money, come to us for it?"

"What do you suggest?" the priest wisely said.

"Well, I think Umberto, the junior warden, is a very qualified person to take this on. After all, he's a contractor! I suggest he develop a plan for painting the chancel and take it to the priest and the senior warden within the week."

The following Monday Umberto called the priest and the senior warden and said, "We're ready! I did some calling around and ten guys will be in the church next Saturday to paint the chancel. We'll bring all the equipment we need, and our families will bring food and join us for lunch."

"How are you going to pay them?" the priest asked uncomfortably.

"Nah, we'll just do it. We love this church, you know."

The next Saturday the workers woke the priest at 7 a.m. to let them into the church. By 11 a.m. the chancel walls were primed, and the workers started to wind down as their families showed up with lunch. Someone brought a CD player, and music colored their little fiesta. By 1 p.m. they were ready to continue, though a couple of them snuck out to take a nap under a tree.

They finished at 7 p.m., exhausted. Umberto, stepping back to look at the chancel, beamed with pride, and thanked each worker individually, shaking their hands. "I knew we could do it!" he said proudly.

Culturally and temperamentally, Latinos are generous. We are aware of our interdependence and connections in a network of relationships. Additionally, most Latinos see the local church less as a place for individual private self-improvement and more as a social center where the quality of our shared lives is paramount. In light of this, it is not surprising that Latinos will roll up their sleeves and get to work. And yet, many Latinos in the Episcopal Church, especially Latino clergy, simply assume that our congregations must be perpetually dependent on diocesan assistance to meet their most basic needs.

It is much easier and more natural for Umberto to ask ten friends to take a Saturday or more to sand, prime, and paint the chancel walls (value: about $3,000) than for him to receive a request for funds in the mail, since the written word is seen as cold and somewhat unreal. And even if he had the resources, Umberto would much rather respond to the vestry's request than to see an impersonal signature at the bottom of a stewardship drive letter. He is more comfortable answering with his body and his time—a much more personal way of getting involved in church, and much more fulfilling to Umberto than signing a check.

Community precedes individuality, . . . identity springs from community before coming from the self. . . . True freedom is not equated with the fully autonomous self, but is found in the relational self. . . . Interrelatedness is the basic quality of reality. —James Empereur and Eduardo Fernández, *La Vida Sacra: Contemporary Hispanic Sacramental Theology*

This points out how silly it is to "translate" or "adapt" Anglo pledging programs for use in Latino ministry. We do it differently. That said, however, there are serious challenges in the area of stewardship in Latino ministry. Years of conditioning, both as former Roman Catholics and more recently as Episcopal members of missions perpetually depending on diocesan assistance, have formed a people who assume that the church is "out there somewhere" rather than here among ourselves. This is true as much of the clergy as of the laity.

In their generosity, Anglo Episcopalians have sometimes been too quick to assume that Latino congregations cannot be expected to be self-sufficient. This is a convenient assumption for both Latino laity and clergy wishing to remain dependent, and for Anglos wishing to keep us dependent through their generosity. It is perhaps one of the most effective ways of managing people who are different, and who, if they were to grow to their full maturity, might do things quite differently too.

Often Latino clergy "in the trenches" (what a peculiar concept!) simply take it for granted that their parishioners cannot or will not support the financial needs of the church. Additionally, when the church budget is so heavily weighted toward clergy salaries and benefits (which are sometimes well above the average congregant's), they may feel embarrassed to do active fundraising. In the process they overlook several things.

On the one hand, pledging is not the only way of supporting a church financially. A mission in a heavily Latino urban area, for example, was able to meet half its annual budget within three years of opening simply by renting out its parish hall for local celebrations. Of course, the prospect of having to pay taxes on that income stumped the church leaders, but once an accountant was found to see to that, the leaders were quickly able to master issues of security, cleanup, rental deposits, and so on. Soon enough the priest handed all this over to a local lay leader who oversaw the project as his own way of contributing to the parish.

At the same time, it must be noted that it is true that Latinos tend to be reluctant to support the church financially, if by support we mean Anglo structures of stewardship, leaving aside Latino ways of sharing and supporting ministry. Additionally, the lack of Christian formation of both new and more established members militates against their developing a sense of ownership of their church and identification with it, both of which are necessary if they are to be supportive. A formation program that is carefully carried out builds up a body of members who know, from experience and not merely theoretically, that they *are* the church, and its ministry is *their* ministry.

Nevertheless, the typically lower income level of many Latinos means that even in the areas of pledging or some other form of commitment, the average parishioner will be able to afford to contribute only twenty to fifty dollars a month. This means that a feasibly independent Latino parish must develop a pledging base of about four hundred families—quite ambitious for an Episcopal parish with only one priest. In practical terms, it means that the priest's ability to spot, support, train, and delegate authority to deacons and lay leaders should be paramount in the list of qualifications needed in the priest. Clearly, Anglo conceptions of the ordained clergy as "helping professionals," dedicating substantial periods of time to individual counseling in an "intimate church," do not do justice to the Latino reality.

In sum, Latino congregations can and should strive toward economic self-sufficiency. In many cases, this will mean developing enough pledging units and other sources of income, which underscores—if for no other reason—the importance of strong Christian formation programs for all members, as well as clergy who are able to spot, train, and support local leaders, trusting them and sharing leadership with them.

LATINO ADMINISTRATION

Some Latino priests—and even some bishops—seem challenged in the area of administration. Under the anti-intellectual excuse that "they didn't teach me that in seminary," some Latino clergy routinely miss deadlines, ignore phone calls, and eventually even retreat from their peers in the diocese, isolating themselves in a cultural ghetto where they increasingly do everything themselves and cease delegating to emerging lay leaders.

At the same time, some Latino clergy are convinced that they will be forever dependent upon their dioceses to meet their salaries—the very people that they treat so shabbily. This is a serious burden both to themselves and to the wider church. In Latin American professional circles, however, this lack of responsibility is not tolerated. Anglos in professional church circles should not tolerate it either—and remember, Latinos expect action from those in power. A bishop, Anglo or Latino, is perfectly within her rights in demanding to know why Father Pedro does not return her calls or show up at diocesan meetings. Clearly, this must change if we are to have viable Latino congregations that are at once true to their Latino identity and closely related to the rest of the Episcopal Church.

This lack of connectivity and accountability among some Latino clergy, however, is mirrored on the diocesan side as well. Bishops and their staff often do not oversee missions and evaluate them on a regular basis, even though canonically the bishop has every right to intervene in a mission church. By "intervention" I do not mean a punitive action, but rather to come in with resources and methods of effective management for the vicar, and to hold her accountable for implementing them. Why, for example, should twenty-three different missions in a single diocese have twenty-three different budget formats? A single diocesan format would work much better, along with a single protocol for reporting finances. An Episcopal mission is, by definition, an extension of the bishop's ministry, and yet we often insist on treating them as if their leaders were private entrepreneurs.

There is an immense need in the Episcopal Church for centralized sharing of resources and methods of ministry, from seeing to the implementation of Christian formation programs to procedures for church administration (easily centralized through online resources) to stewardship programming. Caught in the mixed blessing of being left alone without benefit of careful supervision, Latino priests can too easily kid ourselves into expecting to create everything in "our" congregations from scratch. This only leads to exhaustion and needless repetition and waste of resources.

In conclusion, it may be said that many of the challenges faced by Latino congregations in the area of administration stem from two general sources: faulty training of Latino clergy in the area of Episcopal polity—especially important for those who have come from a very centralized, hierarchically ordered Roman Catholic structure—and the tendency in Anglo culture to expect clergy to be self-made and self-supporting entrepreneurs.

CHAPTER 5

Latinos in Holy Orders

Bishops, deacons, and priests have something in common: all are in Holy Orders. They are ordained, that is, they are placed in a specific "spot" in relation to the assembly of members of Christ's Body, the church. All three orders manifest the ministry of Christ and his Body, yet each one is a sign of a different aspect of our ministry as Christians. The bishop manifests our call by possessing, like the whole church, the fullness of ministry. This means the orders of ministry flow from the bishop and are delegated by him or her at the request of the assembled church: the assembly elects the bishop and asks other bishops to ritually place him or her in that specific relationship to the assembly through ordination.

Deacons are also placed in a specific place or order, a relationship to the rest of us whereby they manifest Christ's servant ministry and the servant ministry of all

Christians. Deacons are of course not the only ones
called to be servants: like all the ordained, they are signs,
and in their case they are signs of the servanthood of
Christ and his church. They manifest this mainly by leading us all into tangible service, particularly to the poor
and needy. Thus they have a specific diaconal charge and
authority: to name what needs to be done and to get us
moving in that direction.

Priests, too, are placed in a specific role in relation to
the assembly: they are signs of the hosting, welcoming
nature of the Christian people as they gather the grain
into the granary of the reign of God. Priests are also, like
bishops, signs of the church's vocation to bless and thank
God, as both do in presiding at worship. Furthermore,
priests and bishops are both called to teach and pastor. As
Christian communities in the early church grew in size,
bishops found it necessary to delegate the ministries of
presiding, teaching, and pastoral care to trusted local
presbyters or priests, as the bishop was unable to be always present in the local assembly.

THE LATINO BISHOP

I begin with the order of bishops, for the diaconate and
priesthood flow from the ministry of the bishop, and not
vice versa. Like the others orders of ministry, bishops are
such in the context of the whole assembly of Christians,
the church. We, the church, delegate our authority as

Body of Christ to the elected bishop, who represents both us as the Body and Christ, our Head. Bishops thus are accountable both to Christ and to us, his Body, the very people they serve.

> A bishop in God's holy Church is called to be one with the apostles in proclaiming Christ's resurrection and interpreting the Gospel. . . . You are called to guard the faith, unity, and discipline of the Church; to celebrate and to provide for the administration of the sacraments of the New Covenant; to ordain priests and deacons and to join in ordaining bishops; and to be in all things a faithful pastor and wholesome example for the entire flock of Christ.
>
> —*The Examination in the Ordination of a Bishop, the 1979 Book of Common Prayer*

Men and women in the order of the episcopate have as their fundamental charge the oversight (*episcope*) of the life and ministry of the Christian people. This oversight is offered in service to the people of God, the *laos*. Even though we are one people, one Body, we are also a motley collection of folks, shaped and formed by different cultures and languages. It is an enormous challenge for a single bishop to serve such a wide variety of humankind in the church today. But this is not new. Bishops in the early church, particularly in very large cities full of immigrants from all over the known world, had the same challenge. Times have not changed, and it is essential that wise bishops today listen to those from different cultures who can bridge the differences between them and their people. Latino ministry demands a particular level of cultural sensitivity, humility, and wisdom from the local bishop if he or she is to effectively oversee it.

It would be wonderful to have a Latino bishop in every diocese with large numbers of Latinos, be they Episcopalians or not. Nevertheless, the few Latino Episcopal bishops in the United States face a double challenge: how to be a bishop to the whole diocese while at the same time being a bishop to Latinos, stepping up to the challenge of fostering and supporting Latino congregations.

Latino bishops may thus want to examine how their responsibilities as bishops to *all* impede their call to oversee Latino ministry development in the United States. For they clearly have the duty, because they have the ability, to develop and implement programs related to the planting, supporting, and developing Latino congregations. At the very least, they must have a strong voice in these matters. Sometimes their monocultural Anglo brother and sister bishops are not even aware of this double burden they carry. Unfortunately, it has become increasingly fashionable to elect retired Anglican bishops from Latin America as suffragan or assisting bishops in the United States, at times working less than full-time but laden with full-time responsibilities and duties for *both* areas of ministry.

Episcopal oversight of Latino ministry
Recently, during a national conference, I had lunch with a former coordinator of Latino ministry. Talking about the challenges faced by this ministry in the face of great opportunity, I asked him what was the greatest challenge he

saw. Without missing a beat, he replied, "Juan, the greatest challenge to Latino ministry is the bishops."

I was stunned. The bishops I know are all supportive of Latino ministry. I tried my best to find out what the former coordinator meant, so I pushed him. "I thought most bishops in the church are eager to have Latino congregations," I insisted.

"Yes, they are, but they think that Latino ministry is simply an extension of the ministry they are familiar with—Anglo ministry—and worse, they tend to approach it piecemeal, when the need (or the crisis) demands it. There is very little proactive Latino ministry development in our church."

His assessment rings true. Some bishops have even told me with a straight face that there is no such thing as "Latino ministry," only "ministry." This tendency to homogenize everything—usually in an irenic effort to avoid conflict—actually masks a covert (and usually unconscious) need to remain in control. This is a very convenient way to ignore the promise and challenge of Latino ministry while honestly claiming to support it.

But can we blame them? Without models or templates for developing Latino congregations, forming members, training lay leaders, supervising (yes, supervising!) Latino clergy, and training seminarians for Latino ministry, Anglo bishops are put in the position of learners, groping for ways forward. This is a recipe for failure. For this reason if for none other, monocultural Anglo bishops will be unable to supervise Latino ministry effectively without trusting a handful of lay and ordained leaders who will teach them, advise them, warn them, and encourage them in their episcopacy.

In sum, monocultural Anglo bishops have tremendous challenges in overseeing Latino ministry when it comes to recognizing when they are out of their cultural depth, how to set goals and demand accountability, and how to avoid working in crisis mode, just putting out diocesan fires rather than proactively and carefully planning ministry development. In addition, the large size of dioceses today has encouraged a tendency for bishops to think bureaucratically rather than interpersonally—a real detriment to their ability to relate to Latinos.

THE LATINO DEACON

Carmen Lopez is a deacon in a diocese in the southwestern United States. She called me the other day, frustrated about ordination to the priesthood, since her diocese does not easily allow "permanent deacons" to become priests. "I have nothing to do at St. Philip's!" she cried, speaking of her parish. We talked for a long time, and I quickly realized that Carmen was a natural deacon. She had retired as a schoolteacher recently and wanted to use her time to serve others. "I'd like to lead people into their ministry to the poor," she said. "There is so much to do in my church's neighborhood! The PTA is a mess, we have no afterschool programs for kids, and there is no immigration counseling worth the name for miles around."

"So why don't you start something?" I probed. "The rector will not let me! I'm beginning to realize that in this church I cannot be a leader without being a priest." My heart sank. Here was a talented, motivated natural leader with a passion for service, appropriately ordained deacon, and she could not exercise the ministry to which she was ordained.

I asked Carmen if it would be okay for me to talk with her rector, Father Quintana. "Sure," she said, "but I don't think you'll get very far!"

She was right. I called Father Quintana a few days later, and found him in his office after leaving five messages (he never returned my calls). Introducing myself, I explained that I was doing a survey of Latino parishes and their neighborhood service programs. He was excited. St. Phillip's hosted AA meetings twice a week, he explained, and once a year they threw a big party in the yard to which the whole neighborhood was invited.

"I was wondering if you had anything like an afterschool program, or a soup kitchen, or a parenting forum, or ESL classes, or immigration counseling—any sort of program directed to serve the needs of people in your neighborhood."

"Oh, I would love to," he said honestly, "but there's only me here and I can do only so much."

"Does your diocese ordain permanent deacons?" I asked.

"Sure, in fact I have one, a nice woman. But she wants to do too much. She claims her ministry as deacon is different from mine as priest; frankly, she probably thinks she is a priest."

I thanked Father Quintana, and went for lunch. I had to get out of my office.

The diaconate in the Episcopal Church is in crisis, in part due to faulty education of bishops and priests about the nature of the diaconate, its duties, responsibilities, and authority. We seem stuck in the medieval notion that the diaconate is merely a step to priesthood, a form of internship to learn priestly skills. Even a cursory look at the rite of ordination of a deacon, however, would disabuse any Episcopalian of such notions. For the 1979 *Book of Common Prayer* draws a strikingly clear vision of what a deacon is and should be.

First, the liturgy for the ordination of a deacon is structured in the same way as those for priests and bishops. This suggests that the three have something in common: they are all *ordained*. That is, they are ritually put in a specific place or relationship to the assembly of members of Christ's Body, the church. Like the other two orders, deacons are a living symbol showing an aspect of the ministry of Christ and of his Body: deacons are ordained to manifest the servant ministry of Christ and his church, particularly as servants to the poor and needy. Like the other orders, deacons are a living image of a certain aspect of the Christian people and our Head: our servant aspect.

Like priests and bishops, deacons are ordained in the context of the church and are made so by God at the behest of the assembled Body. It is *our* will, and not only the bishop's, to ask God for this, as we solemnly agree to uphold the new deacon in his or her ministry.

What is a deacon expected to do? The deacon is called to a "special ministry of servanthood" directly under the bishop, to "serve all people, particularly the poor, the weak, the sick, and the lonely" in the name of Christ.

More specifically, the deacon is to "interpret to the Church the needs, concerns, and hopes of the world" and to "assist the bishops and priests in public worship" (BCP 543). Traditionally, deacons have also served as administrators in the church.

> As a deacon in the church, you are to study the Holy Scriptures, to seek nourishment from them, and to model your life upon them. You are to make Christ and his redemptive love known, by your word and example, to those among whom you live, and work, and worship.
> —*The Examination in the Ordination of a Deacon, the 1979 Book of Common Prayer*

The new deacon will be guided by the bishop's pastoral direction and leadership. The model for the diaconate is Christ's servanthood, humility, obedience. The deacon is to show that whoever would be great must be servant of all. Coming, like Christ, to serve and not to be served, the deacon shares in Christ's service.

Clearly the deacon is ordained to do something different than a priest or bishop. Although all share the same discipline, they embody different things. The deacon embodies service—not merely the willingness to serve others that is required of all the ordained, but more fundamentally the servanthood expected of *all* members of the church. The deacon is not a surrogate servant for those of us who would rather watch television. Deacons are a sign that the servanthood of Christ and his church is a fundamental part of our identity. We cannot call ourselves Christians and not care about the poor.

This is not news to Latinos, who expect the church, culturally and traditionally, to lead them in demanding justice for the suffering of the earth. All we need is a little push—some organizing, some administering, some encouragement and planning—and we will rise to the challenge. Our main virtue in this area is, frankly, that the poor are *us*—we have not yet traveled too far away from them.

In the story at the beginning of this section, Carmen was ready and willing to work hard. She understood her ministry as leading others to join her in service (not doing it for them or in their stead). Apparently, Father Quintana was threatened by this. He saw his work—correctly—as supervising her ministry on behalf of the bishop, but he suffered from a misconception: he saw himself as the only leader, the only servant of the congregation. He did not notice that as pastor, priest, and teacher, his work of hosting and welcoming people into the church, forming and caring for them, is more than enough. He did not understand that he needs others to lead them *out* of the church to serve the world in Christ's name. Thus it is not surprising that congregations without deacons rarely have strong ministries to their neighborhoods.

There is an enormous need for Latino deacons to organize people to address the causes of poverty, illness, and marginalization in their neighborhoods. Latino deacons might be called to get involved in local organizations dedicated to social justice, working hand-in-hand with neighborhood leaders to identify social and economic ills and calling the church members to action. Or they may know and visit the sick and shut-in in the neighborhood (not only sick *congregants*!). They can hold special regard for members of the assembly who must work on Sundays and who have as much right to the Eucharist as shut-ins and the sick. The best deacons not only do these ministries themselves, but they also organize the congregation to join them.

Given the deacon's expected awareness of the needs surrounding the Christian assembly, it makes sense for Latino deacons to write and lead the prayers of the people for the church and the world, relating the day's Bible readings to the real tangible needs of the local community, since they know who is hurting and where. They might also preach a servant's word to the assembly, lead fundraising efforts related to specific relief projects, and work as parish administrators. Frankly, the only priests I know who would not welcome such deacons into the congregation and who are afraid of deacons are those who are stuck in a monarchical model of priesthood, unable to trust and delegate to others.

THE LATINO PRIEST

It may be surprising to many Anglicans to learn that priests were not always essential to the Christian community. "Presbyters" (literally, "elders"), from which we get the word "priest" through the old French contraction *preste*, were originally the members of the Council of Elders of a synagogue—something akin to our vestry. The normative pastor and teacher for a Christian community in each town was the *episkopos* (supervisor or overseer), until a crisis developed in Rome in the early third century. Gradually the Bishop of Rome realized that it was folly to attempt to preside pastorally and liturgically in twenty-three different congregations in the city, many of which spoke different languages. He came up with an interesting idea, one that would eventually transform the structures of ministry in the church.

The Bishop of Rome picked a presbyter or elder from each of the twenty-three congregations and gave him the right to preside liturgically in his absence. To emphasize their dependence on his delegation, the Bishop of Rome insisted on sending them some of the bread consecrated at the Lateran, his cathedral, earlier in the day on Sundays. The local presbyter would then dip the consecrated bread into the wine, thus graphically expressing the local church's acknowledgment of the presidency of their bishop as delegated to this or that presbyter or priest.

I tell this story to point out the deep connection of trust that is to exist between bishop and priest and to explain why the priest in fact has, at a local level, many functions similar to those of the bishop at a diocesan level. The presbyter or priest not only represents Christ, but also represents the bishop, and thus the wider Christian people. Some deacons welcome this delegation of authority to local priests, for they recognize that in working with their priests they are working with the bishop's representative, and they owe special obedience to their bishop. But others resent it, when the ministry of the priest comes between the closeness of bishop and deacon.

The ministry of the priest is similar to the bishop's in that both preside in the liturgies of the church and pastor and teach members of the congregation—one locally, the other in a wider area. This similarity flows from the delegation of aspects of the bishop's ministry to the priest at the local level. So what do we, as Christians, expect our priests to do? As with the ordination rite for deacons, a cursory look at the rite of ordination of priests offers a summary.

> You are to love and serve the people among whom you work, caring alike for young and old, strong and weak, rich and poor. You are to preach, to declare God's forgiveness to penitent sinners, to pronounce God's blessing, to share in the administration of Holy Baptism and in the celebration of the mysteries of Christ's Body and Blood. —*The Examination in the Ordination of a Priest, the 1979 Book of Common Prayer*

First, priests are clearly not ordained to be solitary entrepreneurs, "doing their own thing." Priests are ordained at the request of the assembled church, that "wonderful and sacred mystery," God's family, the Body of Christ. *All* members of the church are called to minister to the world, proclaiming the gospel and working for the world's renewal. The gathered assembly is itself a mystery or sacrament, a holy people in the reign of Christ. Like Christ our Head, the visible Son of the invisible Father, we are to manifest God's glory, following our Head beyond the power of death as the rest of his Body.

In all that you do, you are to nourish Christ's
people from the riches of his grace, and
strengthen them to glorify God in this
life and in the life to come.
—*The Examination in the Ordination of a Priest,*
the 1979 Book of Common Prayer

A priest is the symbolic embodiment of both the local congregation and of its head pastor, the bishop, and thus of Christ himself. The priest is called to work as pastor and teacher *among* the local congregation, not beyond or above it. Some of the specific responsibilities and duties laid upon the priest in the ordination rite include:

- to "proclaim by word and deed the Gospel of Jesus Christ";

- to preach, pronounce absolution and blessing, baptize, and preside at the Eucharist;

- to "love and serve" the people, feeding them with the riches of Christ's grace, strengthening them to praise God, and caring for "young and old, strong and weak, rich and poor" alike, that all may "glorify God in this life and in the life to come" (BCP 531).

Priests in the church today are given a special responsibility to build a *community,* equipping its members for their ministry and proclaiming the gospel of Christ courageously even when it gets them in trouble with the principalities and powers of this world. Priests have a particular calling to shape worship in such a way that it can actually *communicate* the gospel to the local assembly; this cannot take place without deep respect on the part of the priest for the assembly's cultural traditions.

Priests are expected to teach, not lecture. Their charge is not simply to deposit their abundant knowledge into the empty heads of the laity—what the Brazilian educator Paulo Freire termed the "banking model of teaching," but to support the laity's own gradual construction of Christian knowledge and meaning. This requires patience. Priests are also expected to be wise members of the diocesan council of clergy, and in some dioceses they lead the local council of elders, the vestry. In this way, the priest strengthens the people, builds up the Body, and equips its members for their ministry.

It is remarkable how compatible these ordination rites are with Latino cultural assumptions and strengths. The ordained are in *relationship to a community.* Their work is precisely to *build up that community* through oversight, pastoring, blessing, teaching, and leading into service. This is a lot of work—tangible, concrete work, in three patterns of leadership all requiring not only specific skills, but the ability to delegate in trust.

CHAPTER 6

Theological Education for Latino Ministry

A couple of years ago, during a quick lunch across from the seminary, an Anglo priest-friend and I were talking about programs to prepare Latino seminarians for leadership. "We better stick to training Anglo seminarians to do Latino ministry," he offered, "for let's face it, Juan, most Latinos do not have the intellectual ability required to be ordained to the priesthood."

O uch. This true story unfortunately takes place more often than is generally acknowledged. Apart from its obviously discriminatory assumptions, it shows clearly how the power of stereotypes can be marshaled to serve even the interests of unqualified Anglo clergy claiming to do Latino ministry. "Let's not even try to have Latino clergy," they seem to say. "We can do it ourselves." Such ignorant, self-serving hubris speaks for itself. My friend has a Latino congregation of only fifteen souls on an average Sunday. He wonders why.

This chapter explores theological education of Latinos for ministry, both lay and ordained. It begins by examining some questionable attitudes regarding Latinos and education, such as stereotyping and "dumbing down," and outlines a way forward. We then turn to a look at theological education in Latin America and to Latino understandings of education before concluding with some of the operative assumptions impeding the serious development of Latino theological education in this country today.

QUESTIONABLE ATTITUDES

The Master of Divinity degree, the standard for the education and formation of priests and pastors in the United States, is also, under different names, the standard of the Roman Catholic Church in Latin America. Yet I have often been told by well-intentioned people that "Latino clergy do not need a Master of Divinity degree." Likewise, in a visionary presentation of coming changes in theological education, the president of the Association of Theological Schools recently suggested that as the minority population increases, the need for Master of Divinity degrees will diminish. In his 2006 address to the trustees of General Seminary, "Present Issues and Future Hopes," Dan Aleshire asks, "Can the fundamental pattern of post-baccalaureate theological education be sustained when organized religion needs more candidates for priesthood and ministry who are non-white and from recent immigrant families?" It must, as long as the standard for Anglos is the Master of Divinity degree.

This assumption that Latino, Asian, and African-American seminarians do not need advanced theological education points to an underlying aspect of Anglo views regarding the relationship between pastor and people in non-Anglo congregations. In this view, clergy are understood to be chaplains to the laity and thus need to match their educational level to avoid embarrassment. If the laity are less educated, they seem to think, their clergy does not need as much education either. This attitude is worsened by a tendency among some diocesan commissions charged with screening prospective Latino pastors to require of them a program of study that is reduced from the norm. At times these commissions even settle for "reading for orders"—a more or less planned program of reading, often taking less than a year, under the tutelage of an Anglo priest or theologian who may or may not speak Spanish and whose area of expertise may or may not be the same as the reading material required.

We have been there before. In the Middle Ages, the rudimentary education required of clergy created more problems than it solved. Following the Council of Trent, however, both Anglicans and Roman Catholics insisted that clergy should receive formal training in a "seminary" (a plant nursery or seed bed). As a result, our preparation of clergy improved to the point that by the late seventeenth century Anglican clergy were known as *stupor mundi*, the amazement of the world.

"Reading for ordination" in isolation is no way to prepare a priest, for as we have seen, priesthood is a *relationship* to a community and must be nurtured in community, with all its consolations and crosses. And regardless of one's views on seminary education, the fundamental question is, Why is a seminary degree necessary for Anglos to be ordained but not for Latinos? Are Anglos that much more in need of education than Latinos? The obviousness of such institutionalized discrimination is embarrassing.

In spite of several documents and studies regarding the need for seminaries to provide training for Latino/Hispanic clergy, the current situation in U. S. Episcopal seminaries is less than adequate. They have no strategic plan to address this deficit.
—*Creating a Welcoming Presence*

In light of assumptions like this it is not surprising that some Anglo leaders in the Episcopal church have called for lower standards for the theological education of Latinos, usually in a well-intentioned move to "include" us. This is another example of their naive generosity. Explain, however, the nature and normative status of the Master of Divinity degree to any Latino thinking of ordination, and she will protest, wide-eyed and indignant, that she deserves and requires the same preparation and degree that her Anglo counterparts receive.

Worse still, the tendency to undervalue rigorous formation is not limited to Latino theological education. Faced with increasing costs, delayed maintenance, and too high a proportion of tenured faculty, our seminaries are currently facing a crisis. As a result, the temptation to lower programmatic standards even for Anglo students is immense, but not only for financial reasons. Seminaries are at a loss to explain why it takes three years of graduate work to prepare someone for priesthood, since so many priests later complain that "they didn't teach me that in seminary!" Seminary is often seen in an anti-intellectual light, as an "ivory tower" that is isolated from the real world. Thus, besides facing a financial crisis, seminaries are confronted in the United States with a general distrust of intellectual pursuits typical of some aspects of American culture. This is scandalous to Latin Americans.

If not in seminary, how else is a future priest or deacon to construct a body of knowledge and practice about what a Christian community is and how and why to lead it? By trial and error? To my knowledge, Episcopal seminaries, while wringing their hands about financial accountability, have not yet begun to assess their pedagogical assumptions or the theological foundations that support them. In light of this, it may be too much to ask that they also take up the question of whether a single Master of Divinity program, staffed by Anglo faculty, can do justice to Latino seminarians who will pastor Latinos. Yet they know something must be done. The consequences of all this are even more costly than tuition, for the next generation of Episcopal clergy, Anglo and Latino alike, is in very clear danger of going from *stupor* to *jocus mundi,* the joke of the world.

PREPARATORY PROGRAMS

Although there are individual cases where a Latino seminarian must do preparatory work before engaging in graduate studies in theology, as is also the case with some Anglo seminarians, this does not mean that, as is often assumed, Latinos should enter a preparatory program in order to get them proficient in English so they can function in a seminary's "regular" (read Anglo) program. This is another example of the American tendency to think that the (Anglo) American reality is normative for everyone everywhere, thus making them unable to acknowledge cultural differences, including cultural differences in the theology and practice of ministry.

Additionally, such assumptions deprive Latino students of one of our own most treasured resources: the experience of five hundred years of theology, spirituality, liturgy, and pastoral practice in Latin America. As a result, we have the sad spectacle of Latino clergy who do not recognize such names as Bartolomé de las Casas, Rose of Lima, Gustavo Gutiérrez, Leonardo Boff, and many others.

We cannot responsibly prepare Latino seminarians for ministry through reading for orders, or by offering them an abridged program that issues a worthless, unaccredited degree before they can function in the "real" seminary. Their preparation must consist of the same level of education as is the norm for Anglos (Master of Divinity in the United States), but with a heavy dose of instruction in Spanish and an emphasis on Latin American Christianity in respectful acceptance of the different cultural environment in which they will exercise their ministry.

Thus the main challenge in Latino theological education is to develop arduous, sophisticated programs of study, leading to the Master of Divinity, that hold up and support Latino ways of being a church leader. This must take place while also supporting the student's ability to fully engage in what till now has been a mostly Anglo institution.

Hybrid Programs and Distance Learning
Another very real challenge to the responsible theological education of Latinos is the low proportion of Latinos that currently complete college. Only 10 percent of Latinos in the United States have a bachelor's degree. This makes it imperative that we develop proactive ways of recruiting potential Latino seminarians—something our commissions on ministry seem unable to do—and that we develop programs within which students may complete their undergraduate work while starting their master's degree. This is not as crazy as it may sound to those who do not have experience teaching, and in any case it is necessary and can actually be done, as has been proved at The General Seminary in New York over the last decade.

Another challenge to developing competent theological education for Latinos is the distance of some dioceses from seminaries, coupled with the paucity of Latino candidates for ordination. These factors make it impossible for some dioceses to viably develop serious Latino theological training programs without help from the outside. But help is coming, thanks to the increasing availability of Latino professors willing and ready to teach through the Internet, assisted by local leaders of discussion groups and coaches in liturgical practice, preaching, and pastoral care.

In sum, the ripe fields of Latino ministry require us to develop sophisticated programs specifically geared to Latino seminarians who are insisting on receiving a theological education equal to our Anglo brothers and sisters. In many dioceses this requires considerable creativity and flexibility, thus providing, under the spur of necessity, a fertile ground for creative invention.

THEOLOGICAL EDUCATION
IN LATIN AMERICA

The need in the Anglican church in Latin America for quality theological education is enormous. Burdened by scarce funding and left without a clear way to raise up and train future faculty members, Anglican theological education in Latin America labors under great disadvantages. This is not to fault the many dedicated professors whom I have had the honor to meet. Leading difficult lives of penury and limited resources, they are dedicated to their fields of study and to their students, doing remarkable work in a very difficult situation.

In many cases the blame for this situation lies with those who hold the power and the funds that could remedy it. These church leaders and institutions have for almost a hundred years avoided accountability, practically ignoring, in the name of some vague concept of inclusion, the intellectual standards of professional Latin American theologians.

Many Latin American bishops have rightly taken responsibility for theological education, but it must be pointed out that neither their own education nor their meager resources enable them to do so responsibly. The responsibility for theological education in Latin American Anglican dioceses and provinces must be autonomously held by its theological institutions, lest they become pawns of the political and economic lives of their dioceses. This is a very challenging task, as it involves these institutions insisting upon their theological autonomy and academic freedom. Our seminaries in the United States, however, have been faced with this same issue for decades. Their experience and methodology in staving off the incursions of those outside the theological academy would be a helpful gift to Latin American seminaries and houses of formation.

At the same time, even in the United States, in a time of diminishing resources it has become acceptable for local bishops to pull out of consortial arrangements with seminaries of other denominations, under the excuse that they must protect the "Anglican identity" of their seminarians. But this is like insisting on becoming an Anglican before you become a Christian. For much of what is taught in seminary is held in common among Christian denominations, or at least in Anglican circles, with other churches of the Catholic and liturgical traditions. To separate ourselves from the intellectual life of these churches is shortsighted in the extreme.

What to do? In Latin America we might move toward gradually improving our standards to match those of the United States and of the Roman Catholic and other churches in Latin America—that is, graduate study in theology for three years following a university degree. Some will protest that this is "elitist," but most Latin Americans would answer that education is not elitist, but a fundamental right, enabling the poor of the earth to break through the walls erected by the dominant powers. Indeed, we are painfully aware, after five hundred years of experience with exploitation and its harvest of poverty and misery, that exclusion from education is one of the main ways to keep our people poor, oppressed, and ignorant of their rights and abilities. Education is not an elitist luxury for us, but a right too often denied.

Latin Americans value education and consider ignorance a social evil. Thus the shortsightedness of the decision over thirty years ago to close the Episcopal Seminary of the Caribbean in Puerto Rico may be repeated soon, in reverse, as we move apace toward developing a new seminary in Latin America without engaging some crucial issues such as:

❦ the development and availability of distance learning and its promise in a region characterized by long distances and remote locations;

106

❧ our lackadaisical attitude toward raising up professional Anglican Latino theologians in Latin America and the United States, sometimes under the erroneous assumption that Latino students do not need that high level of intellectual or pedagogical expertise;

❧ our unquestioning assumption that local bishops know best how to implement theological education programs and our inability as a national and global church to demand accountability for their decisions;

❧ our remarkable naivete in handing over this project to a Committee on Theological Education in Latin America, comprised by thirty persons of whom only two are professional theologians with doctorates—one Anglo, the other Latina.

In the midst of all these challenges, the Anglican churches in Latin America continue to grow, amid the loud knocking at their doors from prospective clergy ready to make great sacrifices to study as much as they can. How can we tell these eager students that it is enough for them to participate in a "dumbed down" program?

BURDENING ASSUMPTIONS

A series of assumptions work against our efforts to prepare Latinos for our ministry in a responsible, respectful manner.

❦ Assumption: *Monocultural, monolingual, Anglo church leaders know best how to educate Latinos theologically and know best what our aspirations are or should be. In this light Latinos, not Anglos, are the ones who need to adapt.*

Although it is patently true that Latinos must become fully bilingual and bicultural in the United States, it is also equally true that Anglos hoping to serve Latinos must also be bilingual and bicultural. It is of no use to claim that we are a diverse church if by diversity we mean only the people in the pews, not bishops, seminary faculties, canons to the ordinary, archdeacons, deans, members of diocesan councils, and trustees. Members of minority groups spot this well-intentioned hypocrisy almost by instinct. The challenge facing Latino theological education is not, first and foremost, to train us to be bilingual and bicultural. This is a laudable, even indispensable goal, but it is not the main purpose of Latino theological education.

THEOLOGICAL EDUCATION FOR LATINO MINISTRY

❦ Assumption: *Latino clergy will settle for theological education at the level of unaccredited certificates.*
This is simply false. When Latinos realize the Master of Divinity is the accepted standard for ordination to the priesthood, we immediately recognize that anything less is a watered-down version of the real thing. We demand to know, "If this is the standard for everyone else, why are you singling us out for a lesser program?"

❦ Assumption: *There are no Latino theologians available to teach in Master of Divinity programs.*
Not true. The Hispanic Theological Initiative in Princeton, New Jersey, for example, has been assisting Latino doctoral students for at least fifteen years. Almost single-handedly, they have created a generation of Latino professors of theology in all its fields. One only has to call or email them to receive the list.

❦ Assumption: *Latino theological education programs can only serve those who live near a seminary.*
This is also false. As theological education develops distance-learning abilities, theological education at the Master of Divinity level in Spanish is becoming more widely available, making it possible for dioceses at a distance from a seminary to educate their few Latino seminarians through a high quality program.

❦ Assumption: *The recruitment and education of Latino leaders for the church can wait.*
It cannot wait. Currently, of the almost three hundred Latino congregations in the Episcopal Church in the United States, fewer than one hundred eighty are led by

Latino clergy, of whom 60 percent came from various, mostly Roman Catholic, backgrounds in Latin America. It is time for the Episcopal Church to own its responsibility to raise up well-educated Latino clergy, right here in the United States.

TRAINING ANGLOS TO ASSIST LATINOS IN THEIR MINISTRY

One day during my last year at seminary, I ran into Mary, a middle-aged senior, shortly before graduation. She beamed a smile at me from the other end of the corridor, saying, "Oh Juan, I'm so glad to bump into you! Do you have a minute? I wanted to talk to you because I am thinking that I may want to do Hispanic ministry."

"Ay, que bueno! Donde aprendiste Español?" I beamed back.

"Oh no, no, I don't speak any Spanish!" she laughed nervously.

"So how are you going to minister to Latinos?"

"Well, I thought I'd go to Cuernavaca for vacation and take some courses in July."

I wished her well and said a prayer.

Something like this scene is repeated throughout the church more often than most people realize. Generous Anglo clergy and laity feel called to commit themselves to Latino ministry, even though they have minimal skills in our language and cultures. I used to think that this was a peculiarity of certain individuals, but one day, speaking about this to another Latino priest, he said, "Juan, let me ask you something. Would you ever consider doing Chinese ministry?"

"Well, no," I replied. "It would take me years to learn Chinese, and I have no idea what Chinese culture is like—even though I love the food."

"Exactly. Why is it that some Anglos think that they can do Latino ministry by just offering to do so?"

"I don't know. You tell me."

"Well, I have been wondering about this for some time. You and I would think it crazy to pretend to be able to minister to Chinese people, and let's face it, we are not often welcomed to minister to Anglos either. I wonder if Americans think everyone's the same—we just speak different languages, wear different clothes, eat differently. I bet you they think Iraqis are like Iowans—only they speak Arabic. Most immigrants, by contrast, have a much more sophisticated awareness of cultural distinctions and the difference they make."

A lightbulb went on in my head. Perhaps the experience of moving from one cultural setting to another gives Latinos an experience of cultural difference—an experience unavailable to Anglos who have only lived in an increasingly homogeneous Anglo-American culture. Even if this is only partially true, we must take a closer look at the preparation of Anglo seminarians and clergy to assist Latinos in our ministry.

Language learning

Some seminaries introduce Anglo students to "liturgical Spanish" and then send them out thinking that they can "do" Latino ministry because they can preside at the Holy Eucharist in very broken, heavily accented Spanish. But they cannot preach; they cannot listen and understand their people! What leads them to think they can pastorally preside in Latino Christian communities? Are we assuming that a priest is, in Louis Weil's term, "a sacramental stud horse"—someone you bring in just to "do the magic"? Such a medieval conception of priesthood is unfortunately still among us, but everything we have said so far about the importance of communal relationships in ordained ministry belies this. Even though a priest might have the canonical power (and therefore the duty) to preside, how does that priest preside without communicating? He or she might as well speak Latin all the time.

Cultural learning

People who only know one language often tend to think that they can only belong to one culture at a time. Monocultural Americans thus find it difficult to understand that there are ways of being, of living and working, of expressing and communicating, that are profoundly different from their own. But the witness of millions of Latinos in the United States who can live in at least two cultures at the same time proves them wrong.

We are not the same as Anglos. Shaped and formed by other languages and cultures, Latinos have other ways of being in the world. We patiently, with admirable tenacity, try daily to bridge the chasm by learning to live as Anglos. Many of us have succeeded, over many years. We know, firsthand, how difficult it is to learn another language and culture. Thus it is particularly infuriating to be told by a naive Anglo that they can achieve this in a few months.

I have often wondered why our "other ways" are so threatening to monocultural people. Perhaps these "other" ways of being in the world *exclude* them, putting them outside a circle of competence, in a position of powerlessness? We are quite well aware that this is not fun— believe us.

Latinos, of course, must welcome Anglos to join us in our ministry. The fields are ripe with grain and there are not nearly enough of us to harvest it all. But Anglos who generously want to assist Latinos in our ministry must be extremely careful lest the dominant culture's tendency to homogenize, to make the whole world into its image and likeness, awake in Latinos the five-hundred-year-old habit of the colonized to bow and say, "*Si, señor, you know best.*" Moreover, since we spend all our waking time learning Anglo culture, it is very tempting for us to just give up our own Latino instincts and do things the Anglo way. Sometimes this even gets us promoted.

Monocultural Episcopalians can gradually learn to be comfortable in the "other world" of a different culture. We Latinos can; so can they. Even more rewarding, monocultural people may learn to integrate that experience without fear or anger, neither fleeing nor fighting, but contemplatively and respectfully joining these "others," embracing rather than resisting the uneasy feeling of being at sea when trying to engage a different cultural context from their own. This is fertile soil for spiritual growth, as it requires the monocultural person to let go of his or her certainties and become a learner in the "other world." Thus the most important statement an Anglo can make to a Latino about ministry is not, "Here's how you do it," but, "Tell me, how do you do it?" We would love to tell you.

CHAPTER 7

A Vision of Promise
and Challenge

After reading a draft of this book a friend remarked to me, "Juan, you have stood everything on its head!" I hope not. But I do realize that much of the foregoing might raise some hackles, accustomed as we are to thinking of Latino ministry as the ministry of Anglos *to* (grateful) Latinos, or as simply a translated version of Anglo ministry. In the light of this tendency toward homogenization and assimilation in the (charitable) name of "inclusion," what I am calling for is practically the opposite of what is par for the course in the United States: a discovery of and respect for who Latinos *are,* culturally speaking, rather than seeing us as a "mission field" for Anglos—or worse, as a new "market base" that might save dying Anglo institutions. After several decades of dabbling in Latino ministry of the charitable variety, it is clear that the Episcopal Church must turn its efforts to supporting Latino ministries that are grounded in the cultural realities of Latinos. Otherwise, these ministries are bound to wither and die.

Latinos must also take full responsibility for our ministries, both culturally and economically. For we can only be accountable if we recover our agency: our power to act. Thus I have called for Latinos to insist on meeting the same standards of theological training, accountability and self-sufficiency expected of Anglo congregations. We must demand careful diocesan planning of Latino ministry development, and implement strategies that take us away from the current helter-skelter, crisis-driven ways of staffing Latino churches.

We must also address the calling and preparation of Latino ordained leaders, and I have called for the conscientious inculturation of worship, governance, and theological education in the United States and Latin America for our Latino leadership, while holding each other to the same standards that we demand from non-Latino leaders. Similarly, we must insist that Latino ministry not be evaluated by how content Anglos are with it, but by the same criteria used for evaluating Anglo ministry—that is, gospel proclamation in tangible ways, the conscientious formation of mature Anglican Christians, and the building up of a body of baptized ministers responsible for all aspects of their congregational life, including finances.

I am convinced that we can do this. We will have to learn some new habits as we move toward a vision of a church family that includes mature, formed Latino Anglican Christians who are economically responsible, led by an educated clergy and laity, and able to witness to the gospel in their local contexts. Such is the promise and challenge presented by these ripe fields, ready for harvest.

SANTA MARÍA:
A LITURGICAL STORY

Every now and then I write a story about a liturgical situation in an effort to move away from describing liturgy and mission only in abstract terms. What follows is a fictional snapshot of a liturgy in an ideal Latino parish. The congregation's mission is woven throughout.

The short, stocky deacon stood before the main door of the church, motioned for silence, and cleared her throat. Doña Mercedes never felt comfortable at large gatherings. To make things worse, today was the bishop's visitation, the yearly event when ministers of the parish—ordained and lay alike—were officially commissioned and recognized.

Before her stood four new members of her base community at The Kitchen. Surrounded by the members of the parish, they looked at her shyly, waiting for their cue. They were still curious about what made Mercedes and the others feed the street people of the neighborhood at The Kitchen. It was there they had met her, as she patiently—and sometimes impatiently—ran the parish's soup kitchen. Mercedes cleared her throat again and asked them, "What do you seek?"

"Renewal of faith in Christ," they answered softly.

"Come and see," Mercedes replied, gesturing to the four to move to her side in front of the main door, making room for the next group, the newcomers from the base community at The Hospice.

Slowly, solemnly, newcomers to the seven base communities of Santa María Church were asked the same question before the assembled church. This was their first official visit to Santa María, and it marked the first stage of their process of welcome to the life of the parish. They had first come in contact with the members of the base communities some weeks ago, and now, as they began to develop an interest in what made these people tick, they were recognized as Christians and officially welcomed to Santa María.

Miguel, the priest, signaled to the head guitarist while Pedro, the deacon to The Hospice, got the mass of people moving into the church. Only the adult and children's choirs kept the semblance of a procession; the rest went in as a mass of humanity, and the bishop, used to coming in last, found himself surrounded by them all. As they came in they sang a metrical version of Psalm 146:

Yahweh, forever faithful
Gives justice to those denied it
Gives food to the hungry
Gives liberty to prisoners.

The trumpets echoed in the large remodeled church. Listening to the ringing silence, Pedro sighed with relief at the thought of not having to sit through meetings of the remodeling committee. He smiled to himself, remembering the day when the altar rail was removed and the sanctuary extended so the entire congregation could stand around the Lord's Table.

The bishop's voice booming through the church brought Pedro back from his memories, as the newly chosen ministers of the congregation were being presented. Pedro watched as one by one each minister was presented to the bishop with the formula, "Bishop, we, the people of God at Santa María, present N. N. to be and recognized commissioned as a public servant of the church as a ...."

Pedro went through the list in his mind: Graciela as manager of the Thrift Shop. Miguel Méndez as presbyter. Julia Perez as parish administrator. Gloria Ramírez as senior warden. Tomasa Hernández as delegate to diocesan convention; and so on. One was a priest, seven, deacons. The other eighteen were lay leaders.

Pedro sat down for the readings, remembering the day when he had been presented to the bishop for the laying on of hands as a deacon. It had been hard for him to come to belong to this church. He had never been baptized, and had been slowly welcomed, pastored, tended. Part of him had not wanted to join, part did. He kept missing meetings, and some Sundays he would go home instead of meeting with the other newcomers after the service in the Bible reflection group. He had had to go back to Guatemala for three months when his mother died, and as a result it had taken him over two years before he felt ready to ask for baptism—two years during which he had hungered increasingly to belong to these people.

Finally, the Easter Vigil had arrived. That night, by candlelight, he had been immersed in the font. It had been the first time in his life that Pedro had been this naked in public. He had gone in and come out in his bathing suit, and his wife, sponsors, and the presbyter had rubbed him all over—still half-wet and cold—with fresh, scented oil. After they had dried him, he went off to dress in new clothes, and then they had led him, candle in hand, through the applauding congregation to the Lord's Table to (officially) celebrate the Eucharist with them for the first time. And for the first time he had received bread, wine, and—and just for him—baptismal water and a cup of milk and honey.

On the next Sunday he had begun to share with his fellow new members what baptism and the Eucharist meant for him. For seven weeks they had met over lunch, and had celebrated their belonging to this church, sharing their journeys amid laughter and tears. A few years had passed. Today, as he listened to the bishop, he remembered how his sponsors had pointed out to him his good listening skills and his knack for being with people in their pain and loneliness. At first he had not believed them, but eventually, after volunteering to visit shut-ins, he had known an increasing sense that perhaps he should do this full-time, even though that would mean a change in priorities, job, and credentials. After Pedro had talked to his priest about how to explore this, Miguel had set up a small group of three wise people to help him, and they had discerned together his call to the diaconate.

The reader's clear voice brought Pedro back to Santa María. She was reading from Isaiah:

The Spirit of God is upon me.
Yes, God has chosen me to bring good news
    to the poor,
to bind up broken hearts,
to proclaim freedom to prisoners
and comfort those who grieve. . . .

Slowly, Pedro had been able to see that God was calling him to a ministry of service. After all, it had been the church's service to the neighborhood that had attracted him in the first place. Last year he had been recognized as deacon of a new base community—seven nurses and social workers that he had evangelized through his work at the local hospital. He had not been sure about this at first, but the board of directors of the church had encouraged him.

A young girl intoned a psalm refrain:

God has put a new song in my mouth,
a song of praise to our God.
Many shall see and stand in awe
and put their trust in Yahweh.

Pedro thought about the growth of the base communities. There was even talk about one of them, Bienvenidos, electing a presbyter and becoming a new mission in its own right. Their work of protest and civil disobedience against immigration policies had attracted so many people that it was ridiculous to talk about Bienvenidos as a base community anymore. Three groups of twenty-five were cramming into their Brooklyn flat three nights a week to meditate, discern, and plan their action.

All around Pedro people now stood up and sang alleluias. Following their cue, he joined and stepped to the Holy Table to pick up the Gospel Book. He moved slowly and deliberately, holding the book high over his head. Soon he was reading from Luke:

> ...the greatest among you must behave as if he were the youngest; and the leader as if he were the servant.

The bishop began his sermon on the meaning of servant ministry. It was mercifully short, as Miguel had diplomatically suggested earlier, because at Santa María the congregation responds to the sermon. As soon as the bishop finished, six or seven hands went up. Miguel recognized each in turn as they related their experiences of service to the day's readings and sermon and to the ministers being commissioned that day. They brought out stories from their life in the parish and details of their family life. It had been hard training the members not to give speeches during the sermon, but it paid off. People slowly lost their shyness as they realized that being a Christian gave them a voice in church as well as a place around Christ's Table.

As the sermon wound down, Mercedes stepped out to lead the prayers of the people. Pedro watched her as she asked for the prayers of the congregation in her loud, raspy voice accompanied by a wide smile. In her hand she had a bundle of notes given her by people as they came to the church that morning, and so she asked them to pray not only for the ministers, the needs of the church, and the world in general, but for particular petitions: "...for Santiago, who lost his job; for Linda's brother, who is crossing the border; for Avila's neighbor, undergoing an operation"; and so on. People then added their own prayers aloud.

At the conclusion of the prayers the candidates to be commissioned were again brought before the bishop. He spoke directly to them, addressing them by name:

> N. N., you have been discerning, along with your sponsors, how God is calling you to serve others in the name of this church community. Today we celebrate this call publicly and entrust you with the public office and authority of the church. From now on you are a public sign of this community sent by God to serve this neighborhood. You are to help and lead your base communities to become more consciously the Body of Christ and to coordinate the gifts entrusted to the people of God to meet their mutual needs and the needs of the world around them....

The bishop went on to ask them whether they were ready, committed, prayerful, willing to serve all, and so on. He said a final prayer over them, and approached the newcomers from the base communities to bless them on their first "official" visit to Santa María.

During the Peace, Pedro noticed María, the deacon to the Thrift Shop. She had moved to the back of the church to organize the Procession of the Gifts. Soon the people bearing gifts came up the aisle, as the trumpets blared again and the people sang. It was the largest offertory procession Pedro had ever seen. People brought food for The

Kitchen, clothes for the Thrift Shop, and blankets for the Shelter. Some brought pledges to house immigrants for a time. At the far end, Pedro's eleven-year-old daughter brought up the procession in a wheelchair donated to The Hospice.

María organized this sea of people and things, handing over a loaf of bread and a bottle of wine to another deacon who was setting the table for the Eucharist. While this was going on, people continued singing and began gathering in circles around the Table. "Peace be with you!" the bishop said, and pandemonium erupted. The band played and the people hugged and kissed each other as they sang:

No me importa el país de tu origen;
Dame un abrazo y tu hermano/a seré.
[I don't care what's your country of origin;
Give me a hug and your brother or sister I'll be.]

The exchange of the Peace went on forever. Finally the bishop shouted, "The Lord is with you!" "With you too!" the people shouted back. And he sang, "Lift up your hearts." "We lift them up to our God," they answered, raising their arms to imitate his lifted hands in the early church's position of prayer. "Wow," the bishop thought to himself, "this is the most active congregation I have ever seen!"

Pedro, standing at the head of his base community, remembered how awkward he had felt the first time he had stood around the Lord's Table. He had felt exposed, defenseless, and a little silly. All those people could see him! Worshiping face-to-face with others had been hard to get used to. Then he had begun to understand that here, at

Santa María, to talk to God you had to face your neighbors. Over time, he had come to see that Christ was present in the community, and had learned to pray looking at Christ all around him.

The bishop thanked God for creation and deliverance, and remembered Jesus' execution and death for the sake of justice and his resurrection and ascension. As he always did at this point in the service, Pedro wondered if this was what the reign of God would be like: circles of people, all standing equally before God, thanking God with raised arms for giving them a place to be, a place at God's Table.

Communion followed. After a short prayer of thanksgiving the bishop laid hands silently on the many who approached him, just as a Latino father blesses his children, and imitating the ancient church's rite of final blessing by the bishop. Then Pedro sang out the dismissal, to which the people shouted enthusiastically, "Thanks be to God!"

As the people began moving their chairs and tables into the room for the colossal potluck that marked such occasions, they sang:

Wisdom has built herself a house.
She has erected her seven pillars
and has slaughtered her beasts,
marinated them with wine.

She has set her table
and sent out her servants
to proclaim from the city's heights,
"Who is ignorant? Let him come this way."

RIPE FIELDS

To the fool she says,
"Come and eat my bread!
Drink the wine I have prepared!
Leave your folly and live!
Walk in the ways of wisdom."

The Bible Reflection Group

INTRODUCTORY SESSION

The priest in charge of the congregation should be present for the first fifteen minutes of the first session. The meeting begins with a welcome by the priest and an introduction of the leader(s). The priest thanks all for participating and closes with a short prayer, then leaves or stays as a silent observer. The group leader continues with the meeting.

1. After the participants introduce themselves, the leader outlines the purpose, method, basic rules of discussion, and goal of the group:

a. Purpose: To deepen our Christian faith.

b. Method: Active participation, sharing how the biblical stories resemble chapters of our lives.

c. Basic rules of discussion:

- ❦ There will be no cross-talk or argumentation.

- ❦ All opinions and experiences may be shared in this group, however contradictory.

- ❦ The members of the group commit to keeping the discussion confidential.

- ❦ Members may share only what they feel confident sharing.

d. Goal: To become a committed Christian in the Episcopal Church, through baptism and Eucharist, confirmation, reception, or reaffirmation of the Baptismal Covenant.

2. The leader then asks participants to identify the differing situations that bring them to the group:

a. Parents preparing for the baptism or confirmation of a child.

b. Adult candidates preparing for baptism, confirmation, or reception in the Episcopal Church.

c. Adults seeking to reaffirm their Baptismal Covenant, perhaps after a long absence from the Christian church, or for some other reason.

3. The leader then notes that each participant will be assigned a sponsor—a wise parishioner who will accompany the participants on their journey. Sponsors should attend meetings with participants and stay in regular touch with them.

BASIC FORMAT OF THE
BIBLE REFLECTION SESSION

1. Welcome and catching up
The lay leader of the group welcomes each participant and introduces any new ones, occasionally reminding the group of the basic "rules of the game" that govern their discussion. The leader then prays, thanking God for bringing the group together and asking for God's grace to see his word reflected in their lives. The leader asks all to share briefly any developments in their lives since their last meeting.

2. The Bible in our lives
First reading: A woman reads aloud the gospel passage to be read the *following* Sunday. (This gives participants time to reflect on the story before hearing it in worship.) The leader then asks: "I wonder what phrase or image or scene stayed with you as you listened to this story?" The group quickly names these, without explaining or analyzing them.

Second reading: A man reads aloud the same gospel passage, preferably from a different translation. The leader then asks: "I wonder what stories or situations of our lives came to mind as we listened? How are they similar? Different?"

This is the longest section of the session. Each person is allowed as much time as possible, making sure there is enough time for all to share. The leader should encourage sharing, but gently and firmly lead, ensuring that the sharing does not devolve into argumentation or lecturing.

Third reading: Another woman reads the passage again, from yet a different translation. The leader then asks: "I wonder what God, through this story, is asking each of us to do this week?"

The leader then encourages (and may need to start with his or her own sharing, as a model) participants to name specific changes in behavior.

One of the roles of the sponsors is to listen to what the participants discern and hope to change, and to be available and supportive of the participants in these efforts during the week.

3. Final prayer and blessing / sending
Prayer: The leader leads all in the Lord's Prayer or some generally known prayer, and then each member prays specifically for the person to his or her right, as they embark on the new week.

The leader thanks each person for attending, and if it feels natural, dismisses them with a blessing, laying hands on each in silence. (In many Latin American cultures this is the gesture of a parent blessing his or her children.)

The Rhythm of Christian Growth

The Bible reflection group meets weekly at a time and place convenient to the participants. Usually it is easiest for Latinos to meet on Sundays following the service and coffee hour. Other events, such as fairs, vestry meetings, and committee meetings, should be scheduled so as to avoid conflict with this regularly meeting group.

Participants in the group will likely grow through four basic but important developmental stages:

1. Getting acquainted and developing trust
Although any participant may be added to the group at any time, it is perhaps more practical to announce the start of a group soon after Labor Day. After perhaps a few weeks of getting to know some members of the congregation, the newcomer is solemnly enrolled in the parish register during the Rite of Welcoming a Baptized Christian to a Congregation (this and the other rites mentioned below are available in Spanish in the *Ritual para Ocasiones Especiales* from Church Publishing), or if he or she is not baptized, the Admission of Catechumens. In this way the entire congregation is made aware of the process of incorporation through which the church welcomes and supports its new members. The participants join the Bible reflection group.

2. Ongoing listening to the Word and applying it to daily life

This season is the longest in this process, as participants develop the skill of biblical interpretation, finding parallels between Scripture and daily life, making the biblical stories their own. Thus statements like "When I crossed my Red Sea" and "my Good Samaritan was . . ." are likely to be heard. They also develop skills of conversion, trying new behaviors in the light of Scripture. At some point, they begin to say such things as, "I used to . . . but now I . . . ," naming the shape and tenor of their conversion to the Christian life. This is a clear indication of their readiness to mark this change through a sacramental rite, whether baptism and Eucharist, confirmation, reception, or reaffirmation. As Lent begins, they are held up to the congregation on Ash Wednesday as examples of returning to God in the rite of the Call of the Baptized to Ongoing Conversion, or if unbaptized, The Enrollment of Candidates for Baptism. In either case, these rites mark the beginning of their intense preparation for Easter.

3. Lent, or intense preparation

Participants are now on their "final stretch" to Christian initiation or its reaffirmations. With the support of other participants, their sponsors, and the group leader, they begin to name the obstacles to a fuller Christian life that they routinely face. "I have been trying not to yell at my kids for almost a year and I still haven't succeeded!" or "I keep wanting to leave work at five and go home, but I can't stop overworking." They need much support in this period from everyone and especially from sponsors, as they may have doubts or frustrations about their decision to become active members of the Christian church.

This period culminates in the solemn celebration of the sacraments of Christian initiation (Baptism and Eucharist) at Easter, and soon after, the confirmation, reception, or reaffirmation of the new members.

4. Unpacking the treasure

During the seven weeks of Easter the group continues to meet weekly, but now the tenor of the meetings is quite different. They meet to celebrate, enjoying food and music together (provided, perhaps, by the sponsors), and are joined by other members of the congregation who come to listen to them as they reflect, not on Scripture now, but on the rites they have experienced.

They may play a video of their rite(s) of incorporation, laughing and crying about their experience. Above all, they need to articulate what participating in baptism and Eucharist, confirmation, reception, or reaffirmation was like *for them*: "When I tripped and almost fell into the font during the renunciations I almost died, but then I realized I had sort of tripped into this church and a whole new way of living," one might say. Or another, "I was really scared about my body showing, but when I came out of the water I felt completely unashamed, and I remembered then that Adam and Eve, in Paradise, were not ashamed of their bodies either." Seasoned members are often stunned that "mere newcomers" are able to articulate profound theological insights, and as they listen in awe they can reclaim their own baptisms, especially if they cannot remember the event.

The group dissolves after Pentecost. This is important to observe, for it would be counter-productive for the group to continue as a special clique. Some "graduates" however, may well be ready to become sponsors or to lead others in ministry to the neighborhood. This is a time of great excitement for new members, and it is important that more established members welcome them fully and without reserve to join them in ministry to the world. They may also want to deepen their awareness of Anglicanism and the Episcopal Church by joining a group designed for that purpose. (See Appendix B.)

An Outline for "Becoming Anglicans"

This educational program spreads over at least nine sessions that may take place weekly or monthly over a period of time. If participants are used to and expecting "homework," some reading may be assigned between sessions, but not necessarily. It depends on the expectations and needs of the participants.

1. The Bible from an Anglican perspective
Welcome, introduction, and outline of the program. Commitment and registration.

  a. Review the books of the Bible and their different genres.

  b. Biblical authorship, individual and communal.

    c. Finding the original meaning of the text in its context.

    d. Finding the meaning of the text in *our* context today.

    e. Tradition and reason in biblical interpretation.

2. *Anglican liturgy*

    a. Liturgy as the "public works" of the Christian community.

    b. Baptism as incorporation in Christ and not "removing the devil from the baby." (Illustration: prayer in the baptismal rite for blessing the water, BCP 306.)

    c. Anglican understandings of the Eucharist and Real Presence. (Illustration: Eucharistic Prayer B, BCP 367–369.)

    d. Baptism and Eucharist: two parts of a single rite.

    e. Eucharist and community: "We who are many are one body, for we all partake of the one bread" (1 Corinthians 10:17).

    f. Different gifts, different roles in worship: readers, intercessors, ushers, acolytes, priest, deacon, and so on.

3. *Anglican spirituality and prayer*

    a. Corporate and individual prayer: *The Book of Common Prayer* and how to use it.

    b. Signs and symbols as aids in prayer.

    c. Anglican understandings of the saints.

4. *Anglican service to the poor*

    a. Justice, oppression, and the Baptismal Covenant.

    b. Social justice and the Eucharist

    c. The reign of God: Where is it? In the clouds? In our hearts? Among us? The Christian assembly as first fruits of the reign of God.

    d. Social justice and economic and social structures.

5. *The Episcopal congregation*

    a. Its mission as gathered and sent by God.

    b. Who can be a member? Definition of membership.

    c. How to become a member: preparation and initiation of Christian members.

    d. Membership: voting rights, the annual meeting, the budget—how it is proposed, passed, amended, and reported upon.

    e. Types of congregations: missions and parishes, and their differences.

    f. The Bishop's Committee, vestry, secretary, treasurer, and wardens.

6. *The Episcopal diocese*

    a. The role of the diocese and its relationship to the congregation.

b. The diocesan convention; election of delegates.

c. The bishop as principal pastor and teacher.

d. Diocesan organizations operating between conventions: Standing Committee, Diocesan Council, and other commissions and committees of the diocese. How to participate in these committees.

e. Diocesan canons.

7. *The Episcopal Church and its General Convention*

a. The Episcopal Church as a federation of dioceses.

b. The General Convention and election of delegates.

c. The Presiding Bishop's role, prerogatives, and limitations.

d. The Episcopal Church between General Conventions: the Executive Council and other organizational bodies of The Episcopal Church. How to participate in these.

e. The canons of the Episcopal Church.

8. *The Anglican Communion*

a. The Anglican Communion as a federation of Anglican churches. The process of joining it.

b. The Anglican Consultative Council and how to serve on it.

c. The Archbishop of Canterbury's role, prerogatives, and limitations.

d. The meetings of Primates and their role, prerogatives, and limitations.

e. The Lambeth Conference.

f. Administrative offices of the Anglican Communion and how to engage them.

9. *The Episcopal Church and other denominations of the Christian faith*

a. Ecumenical efforts—global, national, diocesan, and parochial.

10. *Meeting with the bishop and celebration*
The final gathering should be a meeting with the bishop, and should include a ceremony of graduation—complete with diplomas—and a festive celebration.

Resources for
Latino Ministry

PUBLICATIONS

The following books serve as a general introduction to the ministry of Latinos. For a fuller bibliography, see James Empereur and Eduardo Fernández, *La Vida Sacra: Contemporary Hispanic Sacramental Theology*, pages 307–322.

Aquino, Maria Pilar. *Our Cry for Life: Feminist Theology from Latin America*. Maryknoll, N.Y.: Orbis Books, 1993.

Boff, Leonardo. *Ecclesiogenesis: The Base Communities Reinvent the Church.* Maryknoll, N.Y.: Orbis Books, 1986.

———. *The Sacraments of Life and the Life of the Sacraments.* Trans. John Drury. Portland, Oregon: Pastoral Press, 1987.

———. *Cry of the Earth, Cry of the Poor.* Maryknoll, N.Y.: Orbis Books, 1997.

De La Torre, Miguel A. and Edwin David Aponte. *Introducing Latino/a Theologies.* Maryknoll, N.Y.: Orbis Books, 2001.

Elizondo, Virgilio. *Galilean Journey: The Mexican-American Promise.* Maryknoll, N.Y.: Orbis Books, 1983.

Empereur, James and Eduardo Fernández. *La Vida Sacra: Contemporary Hispanic Sacramental Theology.* Lanham, Md.: Rowman and Littlefield Publishers, 2006.

Espín, Orlando. *The Faith of the People: Theological Reflections on Popular Catholicism.* Maryknoll, N.Y.: Orbis Books, 1997.

Fernández, Eduardo. "Seven Tips on the Pastoral Care of Catholics of Mexican Descent in the United States," in *Building Bridges: The Pastoral Care of U.S. Hispanics.* Kenneth G. Davis and Yolanda Tarango, eds. Scranton, Pa.: University of Scranton Press, 2000, 81–93.

García, Ismael. *Dignidad: Ethics through Hispanic Eyes.* Nashville: Abingdon Press, 1997.

García Rivera, Alejandro. *The Community of the Beautiful: A Theological Aesthetics.* Collegeville, Minn.: The Liturgical Press, 1999.

Goizueta, Roberto. *Caminemos con Jesús: Toward a Hispanic/Latino Theology of Accompaniment.* Maryknoll, N.Y.: Orbis Books, 1995.

Guillén, Anthony, et al. *Creating a Welcoming Presence: Inviting Latinos / Hispanics to Worship.* New York: Hispanic Ministries Office of the Episcopal Church, 2009.

Isasi-Díaz, Ada María. *En la Lucha—In the Struggle: A Hispanic Women's Liberation Theology.* Minneapolis: Fortress Press, 1993.

———. *Mujerista Theology.* Maryknoll, N.Y.: Orbis Books, 1996.

ONLINE RESOURCES FOR MINISTRY

Church Publishing Incorporated
http://www.churchpublishing.org
   Church Publishing provides the official liturgical
   texts of the Episcopal Church in Spanish, including:

   The Book of Common Prayer / El Libro de Oración Común, 1980;
   Lesser Feasts and Fasts / Las Fiestas Menores y los Días de Ayuno;

*The Book of Occasional Services / Ritual para
   Ocasiones Especiales);* and
El Himnario.

Church Publishing also publishes a number of other
liturgical and educational resources for Latino
congregations.

The Episcopal Church
http://www.episcopalchurch.org/hispanic/
   The Episcopal Church's Office of Hispanic
   Ministries hosts a website that includes many
   liturgical and pastoral resources.

The Evangelical Lutheran Church in America
http://www.elca.org/espanol/
   The ELCA provides a variety of Spanish-language
   resources from the Lutheran tradition at its website.

The Liturgical Press
http://www.litpress.org/spanish/
   The Liturgical Press publishes a wide variety of
   pastoral and liturgical resources in Spanish.

The Mexican-American Cultural Center
http://www.maccsa.org
   The Mexican-American Cultural Center in San
   Antonio, Texas has excellent, culturally appropriate
   Roman Catholic resources for worship and
   catechesis.

Oregon Catholic Press
http://www.ocpenespanol.org

> Oregon Catholic Press publishes *Flor y Canto,* a large hymnal with many choices of musical offerings in Spanish, as well as liturgy planning guides for the Sundays of the year.

The Presbyterian Church
http://www.pcusa.org/hispanic/

> The Presbyterian Church offers a variety of Spanish resources at their website.

The United States Conference of Catholic Bishops
http://www.usccbpublishing.org

> The United States Conference of Catholic Bishops' website provides a listing of the Spanish resources they publish.